# BIG ENGLISH ④ PLUS

T0350561

## Contents

# unit 1 Kids in My Class

**1** **Read and look. Write the names.**

Julia is serious. She likes reading. She has blond hair.

Tony has short black hair. He's very friendly and funny.

Amelia has straight hair. She's shy and plays the flute.

José is friendly and smart. He has brown hair and wears glasses.

1 _____  2 _____  3 _____  4 _____

**2** **Look at 1 and write T for true and F for false.**

1 José wears glasses. _____

2 Amelia has wavy hair. _____

3 Julia has brown hair. _____

4 Tony is friendly. _____

5 Amelia is shy. _____

6 Tony is serious. _____

7 José has black hair. _____

8 Julia likes reading. _____

**3** **Listen and write.**

## Who's That Girl?

It's the first day of school.
We're back in our classes.
Everybody looks different,
And I have new **¹**_____!

Who's that girl
Standing over there?
She's taller **²**_____ me.
She has **³**_____ dark hair.

**In my class are the same friends I know.**
**But we all change. We all grow. (x2)**

It's the first day of school,
And I'm back in my chair.
Everybody looks different.
Now I have **⁴**_____ hair.

Who's that girl?
Oh, wait, that's Marie!
Last time I saw her,
She was **⁵**_____ than me!

***Chorus***

**4** **Write sentences about two classmates.**

Classmate 1: _____

_____

_____

Classmate 2: _____

_____

_____

**5** **Read. Then circle Amanda or Christina.**

**She's Just Like You!**

There's a new girl in Christina's class at school. Her name is Amanda. She has curly hair like Christina. But Christina's hair is shorter and curlier than Amanda's. Christina is taller than Amanda. They're both nice, and they're both smart, but Amanda is shy. Christina definitely isn't. Christina and Amanda are different in some ways, but they have a lot in common.

**1** **Amanda / Christina** is a new student.

**2** **Amanda / Christina** has curlier hair.

**3** **Amanda / Christina** has longer hair.

**4** **Amanda / Christina** is taller.

**5** **Amanda / Christina** is shy.

**6** **Think about a classmate. Answer the questions.**

**1** What's his/her name? _____

**2** What color is his/her hair? _____

**3** Is he/she tall or short? _____

**4** Is his/her hair long or short? _____

**THINK BIG** **Think about a person in your family. Write about how you are the same and how you are different.**

_____

_____

_____

**7** **Listen and stick.**

Donna

Maddie

Joseph

Henry

Sandra

**8** **Complete the sentences.**

**1** Maddie is _____ Henry. (tall)

**2** Valerie's legs are _____ my legs. (long)

**3** My mom's hair is _____ my hair. (wavy)

**4** My school is _____ my brother's. (big)

**5** This book is _____ that one. (small)

**6** Jon's eyes are _____ his dad's eyes. (light)

**9** **Look at 8 and complete new sentences.**

**1** Henry is _____ Maddie.

**2** My legs _____ Valerie's.

**3** My hair is _____ my mom's.

**4** My brother's school is _____ my school.

**5** That book is _____ this one.

**6** His dad's eyes are _____ Jon's.

## Language in Action

**10** **Read and match.**

1 Bob's friends are older than **our friends**.            mine

2 Our backpacks are heavier than **their backpacks**.            yours

3 Your father is taller than **my father**.            hers

4 José's hair is straighter than **his sister's hair**.            his

5 My eyes are darker than **your eyes**.            ours

6 Kim's backpack is brighter than **her dad's**.            theirs

**11** **Complete the sentences.**

1 Juan's hair is short. **Kate's hair** is long.

   Juan's hair is _____ hers.

2 Your class has 12 students. It's small. **Their class** has 15 students.

   Your class is _____.

3 His cousin is four feet tall. **My cousin** is only three feet tall.

   His cousin is _____.

4 **Our car** is big, but your car is very big. Your car is

   _____.

5 **Your hair** is black. His hair is brown. His hair is

   _____.

6 **His book** is light. Her book is heavier. Her book is

   _____.

7 **Their toys** are good. My toys are very good. My toys are

   _____.

8 His singing is bad. **Her singing** is good. His singing is

   _____.

**12** **Complete the sentences.**

> chance    common    fraternal    identical    triplets

**1**   A mother gave birth to Maria and Martin together. They don't look alike.
They are _____ twins.

**2**   A mother gave birth to Tina, Gina, and Nina together. They are
_____ .

**3**   A mother gave birth to Bob and Rob together. They look the same. They are
_____ twins.

**4**   Fraternal twins are more _____ than identical twins.

**5**   The _____ of having triplets is 1 out of 625 births.

**13** **Listen, read, and circle. Which animal can have the most babies at one time?**

Some scientists say the chance of having
[1] **fraternal / identical** quadruplets is only 1
in 13 million. Not if you're a nine-banded armadillo!
These armadillo moms give birth to up to 56 pups
in their lifetime. And every time they give birth, they
have FOUR identical babies at a time. That means
that an average armadillo has a record-breaking
fourteen sets of [2] **triplets / quadruplets**. That's impossible
for humans and very [3] **rare / common** in the animal kingdom.

nine-banded
armadillo

[4] **Multiple / Single** births are very common in the animal kingdom. Often, this
is because not all the babies survive. Cats usually give birth to 3–5 kittens, and
some dogs have 5–10 puppies. These little brothers and sisters look alike, just like
brothers and sisters in human multiple births, but they are very rarely identical.

Other animals rarely or never have multiple births. Usually, [5] **smaller / bigger**
animals have more babies and larger animals have fewer. Elephants have only
one baby at a time. Whales almost always have only one baby at a time. These
animals have a very different relationship with their offspring.

However, pigs are different. They are larger than other farm animals, but they
have a lot of babies. Sometimes they have 20 piglets at a time!

**14** **Look at 13 and choose the correct answers.**

**1** Nine-banded armadillos always have...

    **a** identical quadruplets.     **b** fraternal quadruplets.

**2** How many times does a nine-banded armadillo give birth in a lifetime?

    **a** up to 14     **b** up to 56

**3** Which animal never has triplets?

    **a** an elephant     **b** a cat

**4** Which animals usually have more babies?

    **a** small animals     **b** big animals

**5** Which animal almost always has only one baby at a time?

    **a** a dog     **b** a whale

**6** Pigs are unusual because...

    **a** they don't have multiple births.     **b** they're large and they have many babies at once.

**15** **Read and write.**

| alike | birth | fingerprints | rare | relationship | survive |
|-------|-------|--------------|------|--------------|---------|

**1** You and your brother don't look _____. He's much darker than you.

**2** Red hair is very _____ now – not many people have it.

**3** Identical twins are not completely identical. They have different _____.

**4** Pigs sometimes give _____ to 20 piglets.

**5** Small animals have multiple births because they want some of them to _____.

**6** The _____ between twins begins before they're born.

**THINK BIG** **Number in order from 1 (most common) to 5 (least common).**

triplets ☐    identical twins ☐    quadruplets ☐

one baby ☐    fraternal twins ☐

**16** **Read and choose the correct answers.**

**1** Multiple births are _____ in humans than in animals.

   **a** more rare than                 **b** rarer

**2** Is a big lunch _____ a big dinner?

   **a** healthier than                 **b** more healthy

**3** Whales _____ than cats and dogs.

   **a** more are ancient              **b** are more ancient

**4** Brown bread is _____ white bread.

   **a** good for you than             **b** better for you than

**5** Car journeys are _____ motorcycle journeys.

   **a** comfortable than              **b** more comfortable than

**6** My relationship with my sister _____ with my brother!

   **a** is worse than                **b** is bad

**17** **Look, choose, and write.**

| The Beach Majestic | |
|---|---|
| Comfort ★★★★★ | Friendly service ★★★★ |
| Food ★★★ | Beach safety for children ★★★★ |
| Size of rooms ★★ | Cost ★★★★★ |
| Activities ★ | |

| The Beach Comber | |
|---|---|
| Comfort ★★★ | Friendly service ★ |
| Food ★★★★ | Beach safety for children – |
| Size of rooms ★★★★ | Cost ★★★ |
| Activities ★★★ | |

**1** The Beach Majestic is _____ the Beach Comber. (comfortable)

**2** The food at the Beach Comber is _____ at the Beach Majestic. (good)

**3** The rooms at the Beach Comber are _____ at the Beach Majestic. (big)

**4** The activities at the Beach Comber are _____ at the Beach Majestic. (interesting)

**5** The people at the Beach Majestic are _____ at the Beach Comber. (friendly)

**6** The beach at the Beach Comber is _____ at the Beach Majestic. (dangerous)

**7** The Beach Majestic is _____ the Beach Comber. (expensive)

# Grammar

**18** **Look at 17. Write five sentences about the hotels. Use the words from the box.**

> bad    boring    cheap    safe    uncomfortable

**1** _____

**2** _____

**3** _____

**4** _____

**5** _____

**19** **Complete the sentences. Use more ... than.**

> beautiful    common    expensive    popular    unusual

**1** Twins are _____ triplets.

**2** Identical triplets are _____ identical twins.

**3** The name Kate is _____ the name Astrid now.

**4** Ferraris are _____ Volkswagens. They cost a lot of money.

**5** Curly hair looks _____ straight hair. She looks amazing!

**20** **Use the correct form of the words to make sentences. Make sure the facts are correct.**

**1** mosquitoes/dangerous/snakes

_____

**2** planes/safe/cars

_____

**3** orange juice/bad for your teeth/candy

_____

**4** the Harry Potter movies/scary/the Madagascar movies

_____

**5** sneakers/comfortable/boots

_____

**21** **Read and choose the correct answers.**

**1** Hair under your mouth and on your chin is called a…

   **a** beard.     **b** mustache.     **c** hairstyle.

**2** The hair between your nose and your mouth is called a…

   **a** hairstyle.     **b** beard.     **c** mustache.

**3** The way you cut your hair is called a…

   **a** beard.     **b** hairstyle.     **c** mustache.

**22** **Match to make true facts.**

**1** The ancient Greeks thought men with beards

**2** Prehistoric men didn't shave

**3** Beards aren't very popular

**4** All of Alexander the Great's men

**5** In Europe, beards

**a** in Asia and South America.

**b** are very popular right now.

**c** because beards looked scarier.

**d** looked smarter.

**e** shaved their beards.

**23** **Listen, read, and write.**

> beards   categories   competition   fashion   Germany   Mustache

Some people don't follow [1]_____. There was a group of men like this in [2]_____. They didn't want to shave off their beards. Instead, they wanted to grow stranger or more unusual [3]_____ than anybody else. They also wanted to compare their special beards and mustaches with other men. They started a [4]_____ in the 1990s. At first, it was only for German men. But soon, men from other countries, like the United States, Norway, and Switzerland also started competing. It became the World Beard and [5]_____ Championship. Now there is a championship every two years. Today the competition has sixteen different [6]_____.

**24** **Look at 23. Circle T for true and F for false.**

1  The competition started in the United States.                    T      F

2  In the competition, men compare beards and mustaches.            T      F

3  Men from Norway and Switzerland compete in the championship.     T      F

4  The championship is every two years.                             T      F

5  There are eight different categories.                            T      F

6  The men in the competition are very fashionable.                 T      F

**25** **Read and match.**

1  This man's beard looks like a star. He's competing in the Freestyle Beard category.

a

b

2  This man has a long English mustache. It's white and goes out at the sides.

3  This man is competing in the Verdi category. He has a white beard and a curly mustache.

c

d

4  Look at this man's mustache! It's long and curls up. He looks like the famous painter Salvador Dalí.

**Choose a new category for the World Beard and Mustache Championship. Describe it.**

Category: _____

Description: _____

**26** **Read and number the parts of the paragraph.**

My Best Friend ← 1

My best friend's name is James. ← 2

He's shorter than I am, and his hair is darker than mine. James is shy, and he's ← 3
funny, too. We like playing soccer on the weekend.

I'm happy to have a friend like James. ← 4

**a** detail sentences ☐ **b** final sentence ☐

**c** title ☐ **d** topic sentence ☐

**27** **Read the paragraph. Circle the detail sentences. Copy the topic and final sentences.**

Mr. Smith is my favorite teacher. He's the music teacher at my school. He can sing! He also plays the piano and the guitar. He's also very smart, and he's funny, too. I'm happy to have a teacher like Mr. Smith.

Topic sentence: _____

_____

Final sentence: _____

_____

**28** **Look at 27. Write about a favorite teacher.**

Topic sentence: _____

Detail 1: _____

Detail 2: _____

Detail 3: _____

Final sentence: _____

**29** **Read and circle ear and air.**

year      fair      skirt

curly      pair      hear

chair      taller

hair      fear      more

**30** **Underline the words with ear and air. Then read aloud.**

**1** She has small ears and curly fair hair.

**2** I hear a pair of twins near the stairs.

**31** **Connect the letters. Then write.**

**1** y

**2** ch

air      **a** _ _ _ _ _

ear      **b** _ _ _ _

**32** **Listen and write.**

19

A boy with big <sup>1</sup>_____

And <sup>2</sup>_____ hair

Hears the twins on the

<sup>3</sup>_____.

A boy with big ears and fair

<sup>4</sup>_____

<sup>5</sup>_____ the twins sit on

Their chairs.

**33** **Read and match.**

1 Twins are the        **a** very rare.

2 Identical twins look        **b** common than quadruplets.

3 Triplets are more        **c** most common.

4 Quadruplets are        **d** the same.

**34** **Look and complete the sentences.**

| glasses | serious |
|---|---|
| shorter | straight |
| taller | wavy |

1 Mom's hair is _____.

2 Dad's hair is _____.

3 Mia is _____ than Tim.

4 Tim is _____ than Mia.

5 Grandma wears _____.

6 Mia likes to read. She is _____.

**35** **Rewrite the sentences.**

> My hair is longer than yours.

> His hair is shorter than mine.

1 My hair is longer than yours.
Your hair is shorter
_____.

2 Your brother is taller than mine.
My brother is shorter
_____.

3 His hair is curlier than hers.
Her hair is straighter
_____.

4 Her legs are shorter than his.
His legs are longer
_____.

5 Our car is cheaper than theirs.
Their car is more expensive
_____.

6 Their house is smaller than ours.
Our house is bigger
_____.

# unit 2 Our Schedule

## 1 Look and write.

> eat    go (x3)    have    visit

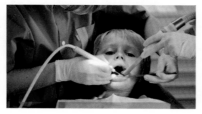

1 _____

2 _____

3 _____

4 _____

5 _____

6 _____

## 2 Read and write the verbs.

1  How often do you _____ to the dentist? I go twice a year.

2  I love going to restaurants, so I _____ out once a month.

3  When we _____ on vacation, we love eating out.

4  My grandparents live in Spain now, so we only _____ them in the summer and on holidays.

5  Weddings are great fun, but I don't _____ to them very often.

6  At my cousin's wedding I'm playing the guitar. I have to _____ a lot of guitar lessons before then!

**3** Listen and circle.

### Things We Do!

There are a lot of things
That I do every day,
Like go to school, **have / watch** a movie,
Stay up late, and play!

But there are a lot of other things
I don't want to do so much,
Like **go / see** to the dentist, **make / do** the dishes,
**Make / Do** my bed, and such.

**How often do you do these things?**
**Every day? Once a week? Once a year?**

I **take in / take out** the trash
On Tuesdays before school.
And I feed our funny cat,
But I don't mind — she's cool.

**Chorus**

 **4** What about you? Complete the chart.

| once a day | I _____ <br> _____ <br> _____ |
| --- | --- |
| twice a day | I _____ <br> _____ <br> _____ |
| every night | I _____ <br> _____ <br> _____ |
| every summer | I _____ <br> _____ <br> _____ |

**5** **Read. Then circle.**

## A Lot of Weddings!

Christina and Amanda are talking about their plans for the weekend. Amanda is going to her grandma's house. She visits her grandma every week. Christina is going to her cousin's wedding. She goes to weddings three times a year. Christina doesn't like weddings because she has to wear a dress.

1   Amanda is going to her **cousin's / grandma's** house.

2   Amanda sees her grandma once a **week / month**.

3   Christina is going to her **brother's / cousin's** wedding.

4   Christina goes to three weddings a **year / week**.

**6** **Now answer the questions about you.**

1   How often do you visit your grandma?   _____

2   How often do you go to weddings?   _____

3   What are you doing this weekend?   _____

**THINK BIG**   **Think and write in order.**

every day     every Friday     once a year
three times a month     twice a day

not very often   ➤   ➤   ➤   ➤   ➤   very often

_____   _____   _____   _____   _____

_____   _____   _____   _____   _____

**7** **Listen and stick. Number in order.**

a

b

c

d

**8** **Circle the correct words.**

1 **What / Where** are they doing after school?

2 **What / Where** is she doing tomorrow?

3 **What / Where** are they going now?

4 **What / Where** is he doing after school?

5 **What / Where** are you doing on Saturday evening?

6 **What / Where** are we going on vacation?

**9** **Look at the questions in 8. Match. Then write the answers. Use the words from the box.**

> eat out    go (x4)    visit

a ☐ They _____ on vacation.

b ☐ He _____ his cousins.

c ☐ She _____ to her uncle's wedding.

d ☐ We _____ to China.

e ☐ They _____ to the dentist.

f ☐ I _____ with my parents.

# Language in Action

**10** **Look at Laura's schedule. Answer the questions.**

This is my schedule.

| every day | once a week |
| twice a day | twice a week |

|  | Sun | Mon | Tue | Wed | Thu | Fri | Sat |
|---|---|---|---|---|---|---|---|
| play outside | ✓ | ✓ | ✓ | ✓ | ✓ | ✓ | ✓ |
| brush teeth | ✓✓ | ✓✓ | ✓✓ | ✓✓ | ✓✓ | ✓✓ | ✓✓ |
| take out the trash |  |  |  |  | ✓ |  |  |
| visit grandma |  | ✓ |  | ✓ |  |  |  |

**1** How often does Laura play outside? _____

**2** How often does Laura brush her teeth? _____

**3** How often does Laura take out the trash? _____

**4** How often does Laura visit her grandma? _____

**11** **Read and match. Then complete.**

**1** What are you doing this weekend?

**a** About _____ a week.

**2** How often do you eat pizza?

**b** They're _____ to the zoo.

**3** Where are they going this afternoon?

**c** I'm going _____ visit my friend.

**12** **Read and match.**

1 Lucy has a lot of friends.
2 Paul's good-looking.
3 This song goes with an ad.
4 This is something I buy.
5 These are big posters by the side of the road.
6 This makes you want to buy something.

a It's a product.
b It's a jingle.
c He's attractive.
d They're billboards.
e It's an ad.
f She's popular.

**13** **Listen, read, and circle. What do children love?**

**Advertising**

Buy it now! Only $2.99

Washes whiter and faster

Michael Jordan's favorite cereal

For a healthy and happy life

When big companies are going to make an ad, they use four things to make us buy.

1 For cereals and different foods, they create a cartoon ¹**character** / **person**. Children love cartoon characters. When children see them, they want to buy!

2 For products like sneakers, coffee, and perfume, they choose ²**famous** / **well-known** actors and athletes. We like to buy the things that these people use.

3 Companies use other ³**tools** / **tunes** for selling, too. Things we can read or hear. For example, they use ⁴**slogans** / **advertisements**. They're catchy phrases we can't forget when we think about a product.

4 Companies also use images with ⁵**bright** / **attractive** colors and great photos. Exciting billboards help sell products because they catch our ⁶**eye** / **nose** and make us think about the product.

**14** **Look at 13. Read and write.**

| buy | cereal | forget | images |

1 Cartoons help sell _____ to children.

2 We like to _____ the products athletes use.

3 When a slogan is good, we can't _____ the words.

4 Eye-catching _____ on billboards help sell products.

**15** **Look at the ad. Read and circle T for true and F for false.**

**1** This ad uses a cartoon character to sell the product.  **T**  **F**

**2** It uses a jingle to help you remember the product.  **T**  **F**

**3** It tells you it will make you popular.  **T**  **F**

**16** **Complete the sentences. Use the words from the box.**

> catch   company   slogan   tune

**1** I like that _____. I can't stop singing it!

**2** Your dress is amazing. It's going to _____ everyone's eye!

**3** My dad works for a big soda _____ in New York.

**4** The _____ for their soda is "The taste you have in mind." That's really catchy.

**THINK BIG** **Would you buy 123 Juice? Why/Why not? Use some of the words from the box.**

> attractive   bright   famous   jingle   name   popular   product

I would/wouldn't buy 123 Juice because _____

_____.

**17** **Complete the sentences. Use the words from the box.**

> Are   going   is   isn't   not   to

**1** It's _____ to be cold later. Take a sweater.

**2** Francesca _____ going to wear a dress because she doesn't have one.

**3** We're going _____ travel to the island by boat.

**4** _____ you going to visit Disneyworld in Orlando?

**5** I'm _____ going to watch TV this evening. I have too much homework!

**6** Zoe _____ going to study chemistry in Edinburgh next year.

**18** **Complete the email. Use going to. Who's going to get married?**

| From: | siennac@imac.com |
|---|---|
| To: | jbruno@doodle.co.us |
| Subject: | Harriet's wedding |

Hi Jessie,

How are you?

I ¹_____ (not be) at Vicky's house on

Thursday because I ²_____ (help) Mom

and Dad. My sister Harriet is getting married this weekend, and they

³_____ (have) the wedding reception in

our backyard. We ⁴_____ (put) a big

tent in the yard for all the people. Mom and my aunts

⁵_____ (make) all the food. Dad says it

⁶_____ (not rain), but you never know!

⁷_____ (you/come) to the wedding? It

⁸_____ (be) great.

Hope you can come.

Love,

Sienna

# Grammar

**19** **Read and write about the concert. Use going to.**

> **Plans for concert – Saturday, July 25th**
> 1 play music – Gail, Tom, Sam
> 2 take pictures for posters – ~~Harry~~ No, Craig and Dan do it
> 3 make the advertising posters - Fran
> 4 put up the posters around town – ~~Gaby and Marie~~ No, Rob do it
> 5 get the yard ready – Gaby and Harry
> 6 Tickets $1

1 _____

2 _____

3 _____

4 _____

5 _____

6 _____

**20** **Write the questions.**

1 What/do/on Saturday?

_____

2 Where/go/on Sunday?

_____

3 What time/go to bed/on Friday night?

_____

4 Who/see/on the weekend?

_____

5 the weather/be good/this week?

_____

6 Where/go/for your vacation/next summer?

_____

**Read and match.**

1 What's the capital of Japan?
2 Where's Libya?
3 What's a good job for book lovers?
4 Where can you usually see cows?
5 What kind of doors do you find in Japan?
6 Where can you cool off in a hot country?

a Sliding ones
b On a farm
c In the shower
d In Africa
e A librarian
f Tokyo

34
 **Listen and read. Then listen again and match.**

a three times a day
b every day
c twice a day
d every morning
e never
f every week

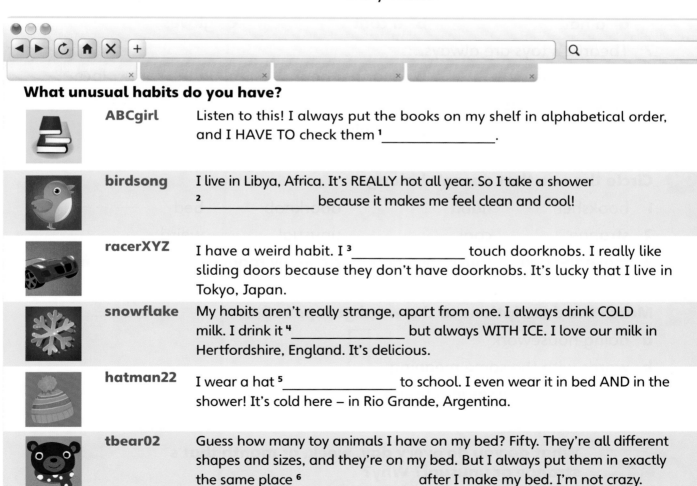

**What unusual habits do you have?**

**ABCgirl** Listen to this! I always put the books on my shelf in alphabetical order, and I HAVE TO check them ¹_____.

**birdsong** I live in Libya, Africa. It's REALLY hot all year. So I take a shower ²_____ because it makes me feel clean and cool!

**racerXYZ** I have a weird habit. I ³_____ touch doorknobs. I really like sliding doors because they don't have doorknobs. It's lucky that I live in Tokyo, Japan.

**snowflake** My habits aren't really strange, apart from one. I always drink COLD milk. I drink it ⁴_____ but always WITH ICE. I love our milk in Hertfordshire, England. It's delicious.

**hatman22** I wear a hat ⁵_____ to school. I even wear it in bed AND in the shower! It's cold here – in Rio Grande, Argentina.

**tbear02** Guess how many toy animals I have on my bed? Fifty. They're all different shapes and sizes, and they're on my bed. But I always put them in exactly the same place ⁶_____ after I make my bed. I'm not crazy.

**23** Look at **22**. Read and choose the correct answers.

**1** ABCgirl puts her books…

    **a** under her bed.    **b** in a library.    **c** in a special order.

**2** Birdsong takes showers because…

    **a** he feels clean.    **b** it's fun.    **c** he's too hot.

**3** Where is racerXYZ from?

    **a** Scotland    **b** Japan    **c** England

**4** What does snowflake drink every day?

    **a** soda    **b** milk    **c** water

**5** What's the weather like in Rio Grande?

    **a** It's warm.    **b** It's cool.    **c** It's cold.

**6** What does hatman22 wear in bed and in the shower?

    **a** a hat    **b** a coat    **c** gloves

**7** Tbear02's toys are always…

    **a** the same size.    **b** near her bed.    **c** in the same place.

**8** Who thinks he/she isn't crazy?

    **a** hatman22    **b** ABCgirl    **c** tbear02

**24** Circle the one that doesn't belong.

**1** bookshelf    habit    doorknob    bed

**2** strange    cool    unusual    weird

**3** make the bed    touch the knob    clean my room    put the books in order

**25** Match the descriptions to the word groups in **24**.

**a** doing housework ☐

**b** words with the same meaning ☐

**c** furniture and things in a house ☐

THINK BIG

**What do you do every day, week, or month that's strange or unusual? Why?**

Every day/week/month I _____

because _____.

**26** **Read and circle the sequence words.**

**My Day at School**

First, we have math class. Next, we have a spelling test. Then we have lunch. After that, we have English class. Finally, we have P.E.

**27** **Read the paragraph. Look at 26. Write the sequence words.**

I am busy after school. ¹_____,
I have a snack. ²_____, I walk my
dog. ³_____ I play outside.
⁴_____, I eat dinner.
⁵_____, I do the dishes with my
brother and my dad.

**28** **What do you do after school? Add two more activities. Then number the six activities in order. Write a paragraph.**

☐ do homework          ☐ have a snack          ☐ _____

☐ eat dinner             ☐ play games           ☐ _____

_____

_____

_____

_____

_____

_____

**29** **Read and circle ir and ur.**

bird
shirt
fur
dear
stairs
curl
ear
hurt
skirt
girl
surf

**30** **Underline the words with ir and ur. Then read aloud.**

**1** The girl is wearing a short skirt and a long T-shirt.

**2** Pandas have black and white fur.

**31** **Connect the letters. Then write.**

**1** s          urn          **a** _ _ _ _

**2** t          urf          **b** _ _ _ _

**3** b          urt          **c** _ _ _ _

**4** h          ird          **d** _ _ _ _

**32** **Listen and write.**

Two ¹_____ with red
²_____,
Two cats with black ³_____,
Two boys with white ⁴_____
Are watching ⁵_____!

**33** **Complete the dialog.**

**Ana:** Hey, José! ¹_____ are you doing after school?

**José:** I'm really busy. ²_____, I'm visiting my grandma.

**Ana:** Then what are you going ³_____?

**José:** Then I'm meeting my mom.

**Ana:** ⁴_____ are you going?

**José:** We're ⁵_____ to the dentist.

**Ana:** Oh, no.

**José:** That's okay. ⁶_____, we ⁷_____ going to the movies!

**34** **Write the questions using How often. Then answer using the words from the box.**

> do the dishes/twice a week          go on vacation/twice a year
> play outside/every day              watch a DVD/once a week

**1**

_____?

He _____.

**2**

_____?

_____

**3**

_____?

_____

**4**

_____?

_____

**unit 3**

# Food Around the World

**1**  **Match. Write the letter.**

| | | | |
|---|---|---|---|
| **1** _____ oatmeal | **a**  | **b** | **2** steamed buns |
| **3** _____ paella | **c** | **d** | **4** _____ watermelon |
| **5** _____ toasted cheese sandwich | **e** | **f** | **6** _____ cereal with milk |
| **7** _____ lamb meatballs | **g** | **h** | **8** _____ noodle soup |

**2** **What foods do you like?**

Breakfast: _____

Lunch: _____

Dinner: _____

**3** Listen and number in order. Which food is in the song? Put a ✓ or a ✗.

## Would You Like Some?

"Come on, Sam. Just one little bite!"
"Oh, really, Dad. Oh, all right!
Mmm. Hey, you're right. It's great!
Please put some more on my plate!"

**Come on, Sam, please have a little taste!**
**Come on, Sam, don't make a funny face!**

"Would you like some chicken curry?"
"No, thanks, Dad. I'm in a hurry!"
Sam says, "No, Dad, not right now.
But thanks so much – thanks, anyhow."

"How about a sweet steamed bun?
It's really yummy. Come on, try one!"
Sam says, "No, Dad, not right now.
But thanks so much – thanks, anyhow."

**Chorus**

"Would you like some noodle soup?
Tonight it tastes really nice!"
Sam says, "No, Dad, not right now.
But thanks so much – thanks, anyhow."

**4**  **Correct the strange food and write.**

1 steamed watermelon         _____
2 oatmeal curry              _____
3 toasted yogurt sandwich    _____
4 apple soup                 _____
5 cereal with lemonade       _____

**5** Read. Then write **T** for true and **F** for false.

**Homemade Lemonade**

Sam makes some cake and some lemonade. He asks Christina to try them. Christina tries some cake, but she doesn't like it. Then she tries the lemonade, but it's horrible. It's too sour! Christina asks Sam what he put in the lemonade. He put in lemons, water, and ice, but he forgot the sugar!

**1** Christina likes Sam's cake. _____

**2** Christina thinks the lemonade tastes good. _____

**3** The lemonade is sweet. _____

**4** Sam put lemons in his lemonade. _____

**5** Sam forgot to put sugar in his lemonade. _____

**6** Write about you. Answer **Yes, I would** or **No, I wouldn't**.

**1** Would you like to drink some lemon juice? _____

**2** Would you like to eat some chocolate cake? _____

**3** Would you like to drink some lemonade? _____

**THINK BIG** **What happens next in the story? Write.**

_____

_____

**7** **Listen and stick. Do they like the food? Put a ✓ or a ✗.**

**1**  ☐    **2**  ☐    **3** ☐     **4** ☐

**8** **Look and complete the questions and answers. Use would like.**

**Linda**

**Drinks**
lemonade ☐
apple juice ☐
milk ✓
**Lunch**
lamb meatballs ☐
noodle soup ✓
steamed buns ☐

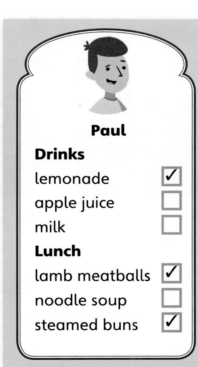

**Paul**

**Drinks**
lemonade ✓
apple juice ☐
milk ☐
**Lunch**
lamb meatballs ✓
noodle soup ☐
steamed buns ✓

**Maria**

**Drinks**
lemonade ☐
apple juice ✓
milk ☐
**Lunch**
lamb meatballs ☐
noodle soup ☐
steamed buns ☐

**1** What _____ Linda _____?

_____

**2** What _____ Paul _____?

_____

**3** What _____ Maria _____?

_____

**9**  **Look at the pictures. Complete the sentences.**

**1**

A: _____ she _____ to have some pasta?

B: _____, she _____.

**2**

A: _____ he _____ to eat some oatmeal?

B: _____, he _____.

**3**

A: _____ they _____ to drink watermelon milkshakes?

B: _____, they _____.

**4**

A: _____ they _____ to try some curry?

B: _____, they _____.

**10**  **Complete for you.**

**1** _____ you _____ to try _____?

Yes, I _____.

**2** _____ you _____ to try _____?

No, I _____.

**3** _____ your friend _____ to try _____?

Yes, he/she _____. No, he/she _____.

**11** **Circle the correct words.**

1   For **a balanced** / **an unhealthy** diet, eat food from each of the five food groups every day.

2   The five food groups are: fruit, vegetables, dairy, protein, and **chicken** / **grains**.

3   Eat more **vegetables** / **dairy** than protein.

4   Don't eat food that is too **tasty** / **salty**.

5   Don't have too many **sugary** / **watery** drinks.

6   **Whole-grain** / **Diet** bread is healthier than white bread.

51

**12** **Listen, read, and complete. Which food can be both low and full fat?**

| balance | bigger | five | grains | guide | smaller | sugar |
|---------|--------|------|--------|-------|---------|-------|

1   We need to eat a balanced diet. That means we should eat foods from each of the ¹_____ food groups every day. The main food groups are grains, vegetables, fruit, protein, and dairy.

2   Look at the My Plate picture. This shows the amount of each food group we should eat. It's very important to get the right ²_____.

3   The vegetables section is ³_____ than all the others. So we should eat more of them than any other food. The ⁴_____ section is also very important. We need to eat a little more of them than protein. Fruit is also important, but it has a lot of ⁵_____ in it, so we can't eat too much. And dairy foods aren't always low fat. A lot of dairy foods can make us fat. That's why the dairy section is ⁶_____ than all the others.

4   Would you like to be healthier? Then remember to always use My Plate as a ⁷_____ at mealtimes.

My Plate

**13** **Look at 12. Circle T for true and F for false.**

1   We don't need to eat all five food groups every day.     T     F

2   Put mostly protein on your plate.     T     F

3   It's bad to eat too much fruit.     T     F

4   Fruit isn't sugary, but it's fatty.     T     F

5   It's better to eat low-fat dairy foods.     T     F

6   My Plate is a very useful guide.     T     F

**14** **Match the words and definitions.**

1   This is the word we use for all the foods we choose to eat.
2   We describe chips and fries with this word.
3   We describe candy, cupcakes, and soda with this word.
4   Chicken and fish are healthy sources of this.
5   Cheese contains a lot of this.

**a** fat
**b** protein
**c** salty
**d** diet
**e** sugary

**15** **Write the food on the plate.**

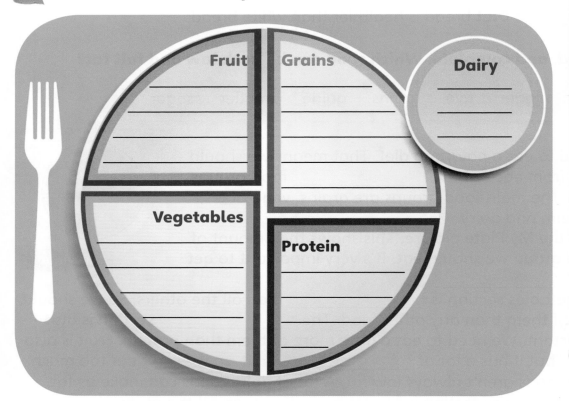

Fruit  Grains  Dairy  Vegetables  Protein

bananas
beans
bread
carrots
cereal
cheese
chicken
fish
mangoes
milk
oranges
pasta
peppers
potatoes
rice
yogurt

**Who has the most balanced diet? Complete the sentences.**

**THINK BIG**

John has cereal with milk, a mango, a chicken sandwich, a salad, and yogurt.

Jenny has a cheese and pepperoni pizza, yogurt, a glass of milk, and some chips.

¹_____ has a balanced diet. ²_____ doesn't have a balanced diet. He/She eats too much ³_____ and ⁴_____ and not enough ⁵_____, ⁶_____, or ⁷_____.

**16** Put the words in order.

1 | dinner | we | Should | now? | have |

_____

2 | Can | go | I | to | party? | Kim's |

_____

3 | café. | go | that | Let's | to |

_____

4 | Martin | visit | Can | tonight? | us |

_____

5 | people? | Should | invite | I | a lot of |

_____

6 | for Francis? | buying | How about | chocolates | some |

_____

**17** Match 1–6 in 16 to the answers a–f.

a   No. He doesn't eat candy.  ☐

b   Yes. But he can only stay until 9 o' clock.  ☐

c   I don't think that's a good idea. The house is very small.  ☐

d   Yes, let's. It looks nice.  ☐

e   No, sorry, you can't. We're visiting Grandma that day.  ☐

f   That's a good idea. I'm very hungry.  ☐

**18** Write How about, Should, or Let's.

1 _____ try some typical Spanish food.

2 _____ I make you a nice hot drink?

3 _____ turn on the TV.

4 _____ making some pasta for dinner?

5 _____ we eat at a restaurant tonight?

6 _____ some chocolate ice cream for dessert?

7 _____ I put an apple in your lunch box?

8 _____ using My Plate as your guide?

# Grammar

**19** **Read and choose the correct answers.**

**Tamsin:** It's Harry's birthday on Saturday.

**Kim:** Oh, yes, I forgot! ¹_____ we surprise him with a party?

**Tamsin:** Oh, no, he wouldn't like that, but ²_____ making him a cake?

**Kim:** That's a good idea. ³_____ help you make it?

**Tamsin:** Yes, that would be great. ⁴_____ make it at my house or your house?

**Kim:** Oh, I'm not sure. ⁵_____ ask my mom. Mom! ⁶_____ Tamsin and I make a cake for Harry today?

**Mom:** Yes, of course, ⁷_____. I have some great recipes for vegetable cakes with carrots and peppers.

**Kim:** That's really nice, Mom. But ⁸_____ just make a simple chocolate cake, please?

**Mom:** Oh, yes, sorry!

1  **a** Let's     **b** Should     **c** Can I

2  **a** How about     **b** Let's     **c** Can we

3  **a** Can he     **b** Should I     **c** Let's

4  **a** Should we     **b** Let's     **c** How about

5  **a** How about     **b** Can     **c** Let's

6  **a** Should     **b** Can     **c** Let's

7  **a** can     **b** you should     **c** you can

8  **a** can we     **b** how about     **c** let

**20** **Complete the sentences.**

> lunch box    main meal    Organic food    school cafeteria

**1** In the U.K., students don't eat in their classrooms – they eat in the
_____.

**2** In some countries, lunch is the _____ of the day.

**3** _____ grows naturally, without chemicals.

**4** Some Japanese children bring their food to school in a
_____.

**21** 54 **Read and circle. Which is bigger in Brazil, lunch or dinner?**

1    In Brazil, our school lunches are **¹small / big** and healthy. For most people in Brazil, lunch is bigger than breakfast or dinner. It's the main **²meal / dinner** of the day. That's why it's important to have a good meal at school!

2    We usually eat in the **³classroom / school cafeteria**. It's a **⁴hot / cold** meal, with either meat or fish. We also eat **⁵yogurt / fruit** and vegetables and usually some bread. However, the main part of the meal is almost always **⁶pasta / rice** and beans.

3    The food we have at lunchtime comes from farms near our school. I don't know if the food is organic, but it's fresh, and our meals are balanced.

**22** **Look at 21. Write yes or no.**

**1** Lunch in Brazil is a healthy and balanced meal.    _____

**2** They eat beans and rice every day.    _____

**3** Food is always organic.    _____

**4** The food for lunch comes from far away.    _____

**5** They eat meat or fish for lunch.    _____

**THINK BIG**

**Which meal should be bigger: breakfast, lunch, or dinner? Put them in order, starting with the smallest. Why?**

1 _____    2 _____    3 _____

_____

_____

**23** Read about school lunches on pages 46 and 47 of your Student's Book. Then write about *your* school lunches. What's the same/different?

What do they eat for lunch in England?

| Japan | _____ (my country) | Same or Different? |
|---|---|---|
| Kids take turns serving. | | |
| Kids eat lunch in their classroom. | | |
| **England** | | |
| Most kids bring sandwiches from home. | | |
| Dinner is the main meal of the day. | | |
| **Zambia** | | |
| People often eat the same thing for lunch and dinner. | | |
| People eat some food with their hands. | | |
| **Italy** | | |
| Food is often organic or grown naturally. | | |
| Kids eat meat for lunch once or twice a week. | | |

**24**  **Read and write so or because.**

> **1** I love eating paella, _____ I have it twice a week.
>
> **2** I don't like eating chicken curry _____ I don't like spicy food.

**25** **Match and circle the conjunctions.**

**1** She doesn't like milk,
**a** so we eat them every week.

**2** It's cold today,
**b** because I want to be healthy.

**3** I often have a toasted cheese sandwich for breakfast
**c** so I'm having oatmeal for breakfast.

**4** We love eating meatballs,
**d** because rice is his favorite food.

**5** Carlos likes paella
**e** so she doesn't drink it.

**6** I eat a balanced diet
**f** because I like cheese a lot.

**26** **Join the sentences and write. Use so and because.**

**1** I'm wearing a coat. It's cold.

_____

**2** I don't like fruit. I don't eat watermelon.

_____

**3** Sally is happy. She's eating her favorite lunch.

_____

**27** **Read and circle** le, el, al, **and** il.

> apple    curl    April
>
> pencil    medal    sandal
>
> hear    camel    hair
>
> bubble    travel

**28** **Underline the words with** le, el, al, **and** il. **Then read aloud.**

**1** There are apples in April.

**2** I wear sandals when I travel in the summer.

**29** **Connect the letters. Then write.**

**1** app          el          **a** _ _ _ _ _

**2** Apr          le          **b** _ _ _ _ _

**3** cam          al          **c** _ _ _ _ _

**4** med          il          **d** _ _ _ _ _

**30** **Listen and write.**

60

Take your ¹ _____ .
Draw a ² _____ .
Draw a ³ _____ .
Draw some ⁴ _____ .

**31** **Write questions or answers.**

**1** What would she like for breakfast?

_____

**2** _____

He'd like a toasted cheese sandwich for lunch.

**3** What would they like for dinner?

_____

**4** _____

They'd like chicken curry for dinner.

**5** What would you like for dinner?

_____

**32** **Read and circle.**

**Mom:** ¹**Would / Should** you like to go to an Indian restaurant?

**Bobby:** No, I ²**can't / wouldn't**.

**Mom:** ³**Let's / How about** an Italian restaurant?

**Bobby:** No, ⁴**let's / thanks**.

**Mom:** Well, where ⁵**can / would** you like to go?

**Bobby:** ⁶**I'd like / Let's go** to a candy store!

**33** **Read and match.**

1 Eat more grains        **a** balanced diet.

2 Don't eat too          **b** much salt.

3 Have a lot of          **c** than protein.

4 Have a                 **d** fruit.

# My Robot

**1** **Choose and draw one path. Design a robot.**

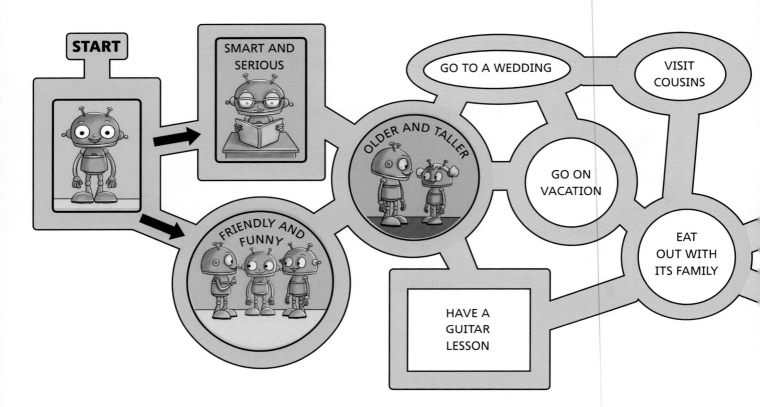

**2** **Look at your path in 1. Answer the questions with words from your path.**

What is the robot like? _____ _____ _____

What is it doing today? _____ _____ _____

What would it like to try? _____ _____ _____

**3** **Look at your path in 1 and ✓ the word or words.**

My robot likes ☐ spicy ☐ salty ☐ sweet ☐ sour food.

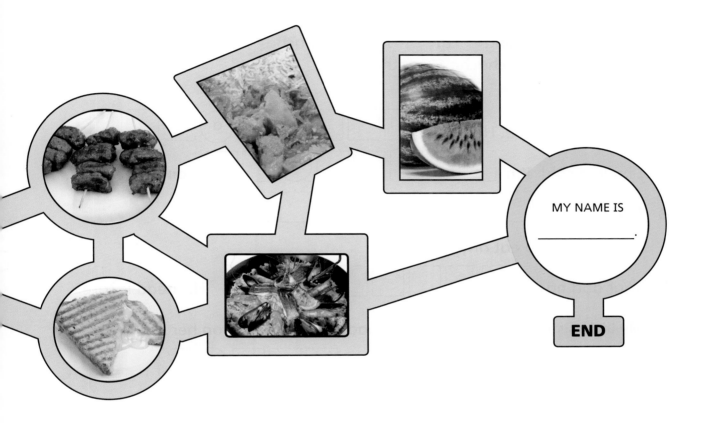

MY NAME IS

_____.

END

**4** **Look at the information about your robot. Give it a name.
Write a paragraph about it.**

_____

_____

_____

_____

_____

_____

# unit 4 How Do You Feel?

**1** **Complete the sentences.**

> allergies   coughing   cut   fever   headache
> sneezing   stomachache   toothache

**1** His teeth are sore. He has a ⬜⬜⬜⬜⬜ⓐ⬜⬜⬜ .

**2** I have a cold. I'm ⬜⬜⬜⬜⬜⭕⬜⬜ , and I feel tired.

**3** I have a ⭕⬜⬜⬜⬜⬜⬜⬜⬜⬜⬜ .
I don't want to eat anything.

**4** Your dad has a ⬜⬜⬜⬜⬜⭕⬜⬜ . His head is sore.

**5** My little sister fell. Now she has a bad ⬜ⓤ⬜ on her leg.

**6** Your head feels hot. You must have a ⬜⬜⬜⭕⬜ .

**7** My mom has bad ⬜⭕⬜⬜⬜⬜⬜⬜⬜ . She's
⬜⬜⭕⬜⬜⬜⭕⬜ a lot.

**2** **Write the letters from the circles in 1. Use the letters to complete the joke.**

ⓐ ⭕ ⭕ ⭕ ⓤ ⭕ ⭕ ⭕ ⭕

Doctor, my son ate my pen! What should I do?

ⓤ ⭕ ⭕ ⓐ
p ⭕ ⭕ ⭕ ⭕ ⭕

**3** **Listen and write. Use the words from the box.**

## Stay in Bed and Rest!

You're ¹_____
And you're ²_____.
You need to stay in bed.
I think you have a fever.
Here, let me feel your head.
You shouldn't go to school today.
You should ³_____ instead.

**When you're sick or feeling blue,
Your family takes good care of you.**

You have a ⁴_____
And a ⁵_____.
Here's what I suggest:
You should drink some ⁶_____
And juice.
⁷_____ and rest!
Listen to your dad, now,
Taking care of yourself is best.

**Chorus**

cold    coughing    fever
sneezing    stay home
stay in bed    tea

**4** **Read and choose the correct answers.**

When you're sick, here's what I suggest:

**1** You shouldn't…
   **a** stay in bed.  **b** go to school.  **c** stay home.

**2** You shouldn't…
   **a** run around.  **b** rest.  **c** drink water.

**3** You shouldn't…
   **a** go to a doctor.  **b** eat candy.  **c** take care of yourself.

**5** **Read. Then answer the questions.**

You're Hurt!

Sam and Christina are having lunch together. Sam sees something red on Christina's arm. He gets upset because he thinks Christina has a cut. He tells Christina that she should see the nurse and put a bandage on her arm. But Christina tells him that it's not blood on her arm – it's ketchup! She's OK, but she needs a napkin.

**1** What are Sam and Christina doing? _____

**2** Who does Sam think Christina should see? _____

**3** What does Sam think Christina should do? _____

**6** **Read. Then complete the sentences.**

nurse   bandage   rest   run

I fell and cut my knee. Ouch!

You should _____
_____.
_____.
You shouldn't _____.

**THINK BIG** **Look at 5 again. What happens next in the story? Write.**

_____

_____

**7** **Listen and stick. Number in order and write.**

**a**

He should go to the _____.

**b**

She should go to the _____.

**c**

She should take some _____.

**d**

He should eat some soup and get some _____.

**8** **Read and circle.**

1  I **should** / **shouldn't** eat vegetables.

2  He **should** / **shouldn't** exercise every day.

3  We **should** / **shouldn't** stay up late.

4  They **should** / **shouldn't** eat healthy food.

**9** **Read and write should or shouldn't.**

1  **Joe:**  I have a headache.

   **Doctor:**  You _____ drink some water.

2  **Dad:**  My children have allergies.

   **Doctor:**  They _____ stay inside and take medicine.

3  **Mom:**  My son has a fever.

   **Doctor:**  He _____ go to school.

4  **Sonya:**  I like watching TV for hours every day.

   **Doctor:**  You _____ watch so much TV.

## Language in Action

**10** **Read and ✓ the correct answers.**

**1** I go to bed late and eat a lot of chips. I should take better care of _____.

**a** ☐ myself     **b** ☐ yourself     **c** ☐ herself

**2** You never eat fruit. You should take better care of _____.

**a** ☐ myself     **b** ☐ yourself     **c** ☐ ourselves

**3** She exercises a lot. She takes good care of _____.

**a** ☐ himself     **b** ☐ themselves   **c** ☐ herself

**4** We eat a healthy breakfast. We take good care of _____.

**a** ☐ myself     **b** ☐ ourselves     **c** ☐ themselves

**5** They watch TV all the time. They should take better care of _____.

**a** ☐ themselves    **b** ☐ ourselves     **c** ☐ herself

**6** He always washes his hands. He takes good care of _____.

**a** ☐ herself     **b** ☐ myself     **c** ☐ himself

**11** **Read the problems. Write advice.**

**1** I'm coughing, and I have a sore throat.

_____

**2** My brother has a cut on his leg.

_____

**3** My friends don't eat vegetables.

_____

**4** I have a stomachache.

_____

**5** I stay up late every night.

_____

**12** **Listen, read, and complete. When should we use tissues?**

clean    dirty water    diseases    enemies
microscope    Protect    spread    toothbrush

**1** **About Germs**
We try to stay healthy, but there are tiny
¹ _____ all around us called germs. They're always there, but we can only see them with a ² _____.
Unfortunately, they can cause
³ _____.

**2** **Where Are Germs?**
They are everywhere. In the air, on old food, in
⁴ _____, and on everything we touch with our dirty hands: the sink, the bathtub, our
⁵ _____, the TV remote control, and our computer keyboards.

**3** **Kinds of Germs**
There isn't just one kind of germ, there are at least four. Each one is a little different. The main ones are bacteria, viruses, fungi, and protozoa.

**4** **How Do We**
⁶ _____ **Ourselves?**
We can wash our hands often and keep the house
⁷ _____. When we have a cold or a cough, we should use tissues. Also, we should stay at home, so our germs don't
⁸ _____.

**13** **Read and answer.**

**1** How many kinds of germs are there?    _____

**2** Can germs make us sick?    _____

**3** Write three ways germs can get into the home.

_____

**4** Write three ways we can stay away from germs.

_____

**14** **Match. Look at page 64 of your Student's Book.**

1 virus

a

b

2 bacteria

3 fungi

c

d

4 protozoa

**15** **Write germs 1–4 next to the information. Use the text on page 64 of your Student's Book.**

1 They grow on old food. _____ _____

2 They live in dirty water. _____

3 It's in the air and gives us coughs and colds. _____

4 The disease malaria comes from this. _____

5 They're sometimes good and help us digest food. _____

6 It can spread quickly through sneezes. _____

THINK BIG

**Think and ✓ or ✗. Can you find germs on a...?**

library book ☐    computer mouse ☐    toilet ☐    coin ☐

phone ☐    door ☐    toy ☐    water fountain ☐

Which do you think has the most germs? Why?

_____

_____

**16** **Read and write questions and short answers with should and shouldn't.**

**A**

Mom didn't put the meat in the fridge. It was out of the fridge all night!

**1** eat/they/the meat?

_____

No, they _____.

**2** throw/they/the meat in the trash?

_____

Yes, they _____.

**B**

Dad has a really bad cold. But he has an important meeting at work.

**3** go/he/to work?

_____

_____

**4** stay/he/home today?

_____

_____

**C**

Amalia and Denise found a handbag in the street. They are deciding what to do.

**5** keep/we/the handbag?

_____

_____

**6** take/we/it to the police?

_____

_____

**D**

Marlena has an important exam tomorrow.

**7** study/she/all night?

_____

_____

**8** go/she/to bed without studying?

_____

_____

**17** **Look at 16 and match A–D to four of the suggestions below. Write sentences with could.**

- give the meat to the cat
- use the computer to take part in the meeting
- eat the meat tonight

- look for a phone number in the handbag
- get up early and study
- give the handbag to their mom
- not sleep tonight

**1** _____

**2** _____

**3** _____

**4** _____

# Grammar

**18** **Make six questions with should. Write them in your notebook.**

| How | | go | in your city? |
|---|---|---|---|
| What | | do | for a sore throat? |
| Where | people | travel | in your city or country? |
| When | | spend time | on a rainy day? |
| | | wear | to weddings? |
| | | use | cell phones? |

**19** **Use the prompts, or your own ideas, to write suggestions. Use could.**

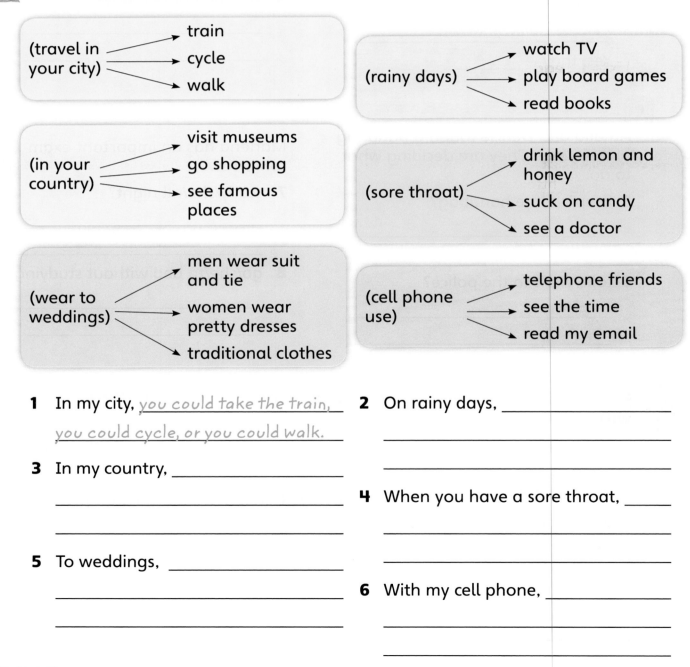

(travel in your city) → train → cycle → walk

(rainy days) → watch TV → play board games → read books

(in your country) → visit museums → go shopping → see famous places

(sore throat) → drink lemon and honey → suck on candy → see a doctor

(wear to weddings) → men wear suit and tie → women wear pretty dresses → traditional clothes

(cell phone use) → telephone friends → see the time → read my email

**1** In my city, <u>you could take the train,</u> <u>you could cycle, or you could walk.</u>

**2** On rainy days, _____

_____

_____

**3** In my country, _____

_____

_____

**4** When you have a sore throat, _____

_____

_____

**5** To weddings, _____

_____

**6** With my cell phone, _____

_____

_____

**20** **Read and choose the correct answers.**

**1** Doctors don't have a _____ for everything.

   **a** benefit      **b** cure      **c** home remedy

**2** Many doctors tell you to take _____ for a headache.

   **a** painkillers      **b** vinegar      **c** ingredients

**3** Tea is one of the oldest _____.

   **a** medicines      **b** home remedies      **c** illnesses

**4** Hot chicken soup has many health _____.

   **a** remedies      **b** benefits      **c** cures

**21** 76 **Listen, read, and circle. Then write the correct remedy.**

Cinnamon    Garlic    Ginger

http://www.remediesrus.com

1 _____ is used around the world as a home remedy for many different problems. For example, many people take it when they have a [1] **headache / stomachache**. In Japan, mothers give their children ginger tea with sugar when they have a [2] **cough / cold**. In Europe, people drink it in hot water with honey and lemon to help with sore throats.

2 _____ is also a common home remedy. In Spain, people add it to their tea to help with colds and coughs. Some Native Americans put it on [3] **mosquito / bee** stings. It helps stop the sting from hurting.

3 _____ is another common home remedy. Many people use it for colds, but did you know you can also use it to help with a [4] **toothache / backache**? Just mix some with honey and put it on the sore tooth. This not only helps the tooth hurt less, but also [5] **smells / tastes** delicious.

**22** **Look at 21 and ✓.**

|  | bee sting | cold | sore throat | stomachache | toothache |
|---|---|---|---|---|---|
| ginger |  |  |  |  |  |
| garlic |  |  |  |  |  |
| cinnamon |  |  |  |  |  |

**23** **Match.**

**1** A relaxing drink. Sometimes it's a home remedy for sore throats.

**2** When you rub someone to help them relax.

**3** Sleep is the best way to do this.

**4** When you have a fever, this makes your body feel cooler.

**5** You feel this before exams and during difficult times.

**a** herbal tea

**b** rest

**c** massage

**d** stress

**e** vinegar

**THINK BIG**

**These are some common illnesses around the world. Write HR when should you use a home remedy or D when should you go to the doctor.**

allergies ☐    malaria ☐    vomiting ☐    sore throat ☐

headache ☐    back pain ☐    cold ☐    cough ☐

high fever ☐    bad cut ☐

Are there any illnesses for which you should do both? Why?

_____

_____

**24**  **Are commas used correctly? Read and ✓ or ✗.**

**1 a** First, I eat a healthy breakfast. Then I go swimming.

  **b** First I eat a healthy breakfast. Then, I go swimming.

**2 a** You should drink some tea take some medicine and sleep.

  **b** You should drink some tea, take some medicine, and sleep.

**3 a** I take good care of myself. She takes good care of herself too.

  **b** I take good care of myself. She takes good care of herself, too.

**25** **Add commas in the correct places.**

**1** I get a lot of rest drink water exercise and eat fruit.

**2** I don't eat cookies cake chocolate or candy.

**3** First I should eat a healthy dinner. Then I should do my homework. Finally I should go to bed.

**4** The four kinds of germs are bacteria fungi protozoa and viruses.

**5** You should drink some tea. You should take some medicine too.

**6** First he should take some medicine. After that he should have some soup.

**26** **Write answers. Remember to use commas.**

**1** I want to eat a healthy lunch. What should I eat?

_____

_____

**2** I want to be healthy and exercise. What should I do?

_____

_____

**3** I have a stomachache and a fever. What should I do?

_____

_____

**27** **Read and circle kn and wr.**

knee    breakfast    wrist
knight    write    wrong
know    knock    right
now    wrap

**28** **Underline the words with kn and wr. Then read aloud.**

**1** The knight knows how to write.

**2** He wraps his knee and knots the rope.

**29** **Connect the letters. Then write.**

**1** kn                    eck        **a** _ _ _ _ _

**2** wr                    ock        **b** _ _ _ _ _

**30** **Listen and write.**

81

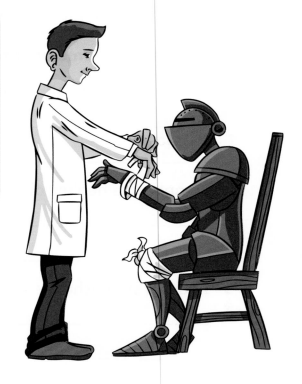

What's wrong, ¹_____, wrong?
The ²_____ knocked his
Knee, knee, knee,
And his wrist, wrist, ³_____.
I ⁴_____! Wrap his knee
And ⁵_____ his wrist!

**31** **Read and match.**

1 We have to
2 Germs make
3 Bacteria is
4 Germs get into

a one kind of germ.
b many places.
c protect ourselves from germs.
d a kind of poison called a toxin.

**32** **Read and circle.**

1 She stays up late every night. She should take better care of **himself / herself**.
2 They take good care of **themselves / ourselves**. They exercise every morning.
3 I eat a lot of chips. I should take better care of **myself / yourself**.
4 You always eat a healthy lunch. You take good care of **yourself / ourselves**.

**33** **Look and write. Then complete the sentences with should or shouldn't.**

| allergies    cut    fever    headache    sore throat    stomachache |

1 She has a _____. She _____ drink water and rest.

2 He has a _____. He _____ talk too much.

3 She has a _____. She _____ go to school.

4 He has a _____. He _____ eat so much candy.

5 She has _____. She _____ go outside.

6 He has a _____. He _____ take better care of himself.

# Weird and Wild Animals

 **1** **Look and write. Then match.**

angler fish   coconut crabs   tarsiers   Tasmanian devils   volcano rabbits

**1** _____

**2** _____

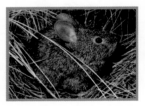

**3** _____

**4** _____

**5** _____

**a** They have long teeth, and they live in oceans all over the world. We don't know how many there are.

**b** They have big eyes and brown fur. They live in Southeast Asia, but we don't know their population.

**c** They have a population of more than 100,000, and they live on islands in the Pacific Ocean. They're orange and brown.

**d** They have gray fur, and they live on volcanoes in Mexico. They have a population of between 2,000 and 12,000.

**e** They have black and white fur. They have a population of between 10,000 and 25,000, and you can find them in Tasmania.

**2** **Listen and write. Then draw.**

♪ Understanding Animals ♪

Do you know a lot about animals?
How many different kinds there are.
Some are **1** _____, and
Some are **2** _____,
And some are just bizarre!

**Understanding animals is good for us to do**
**Because learning about animals helps us**
**And helps them, too!**

Some live in **3** _____, or in the
**4** _____,
And some live where it's hot.
Some are beautiful, and some are cute,
And some are... well, they're not!

**Chorus**

It's important to learn about animals,
Though many seem strange, it's true.
Because when we learn about animals,
We learn about ourselves, too.

**Chorus**

**3** **Write the animals.**

| big | small | live in trees | live in the ocean |
|-----|-------|---------------|-------------------|
|     |       |               |                   |
|     |       |               |                   |
|     |       |               |                   |

**4** **Read. Then complete the sentences.**

**Chimps Are Smart!**

Christina is watching a TV program about chimpanzees. She learns that chimps are smart and amazing animals. They can climb trees, talk to other chimps, and use tools to get food. But there are not many chimps left in the wild. They are endangered because people are moving into their habitat. Sam can talk, climb trees, and use tools to get food, too. He hopes he isn't endangered!

**1** Christina is watching a program about _____, or chimps.

**2** Chimps are _____ and amazing animals.

**3** They can climb trees and _____ to each other.

**4** Chimps use _____ to get food.

**5** There aren't many chimps in the wild – they're _____.

**5** **Answer about you.**

**1** Can you do any of the things that chimps can do?

_____

**2** Do you like chimps? Why/Why not?

_____

**THINK BIG** **Chimps use tools to get food. What tools do you use to...**

**a** cook/eat food?           _____

**b** do your homework?      _____

**c** stay clean?             _____

**6** **Listen and stick. Then write.**

**1**

**2**

**3**

1990s: more than 100,000

Now: _____

100 years ago: about 100,000

Now: _____

100 years ago: about 90,000

Now: _____

**7** **Read and complete.**

| | | **There were...** | **There are...** |
|---|---|---|---|
| | Komodo dragon | How many? *more than 20,000*<br>When? *fifty years ago* | How many? *fewer than 5,000*<br>When? *now* |
| | Andean condor | How many? *a lot*<br>When? *in the past* | How many? *about 10,000*<br>When? *now* |
| | Tasmanian devil | How many? *100,000*<br>When? *twenty-five years ago* | How many? *between 10,000 and 25,000*<br>When? *now* |

**1**  **A:** _____ [_____] _____ in the past?

   **B:** _____ a lot. Now _____ about 10,000.

**2**  **A:** _____ [_____] _____ twenty-five

   years ago?

   **B:** _____ 100,000. Now _____ between 10,000
   and 25,000.

**3**  **A:** _____ [_____] _____ fifty years ago?

   **B:** _____ more than 20,000. Now _____ fewer than 5,000.

**8** Why are they endangered? Follow each maze and complete the dialogs.

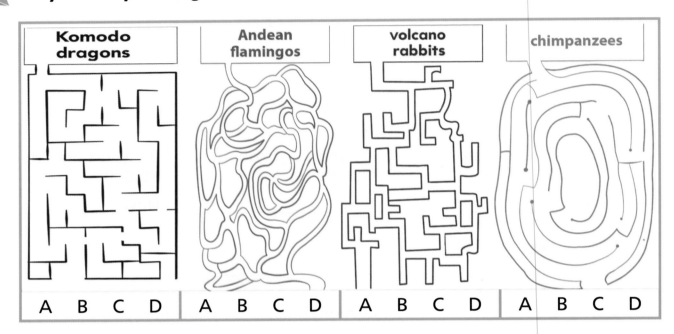

Komodo dragons    A B C D

Andean flamingos    A B C D

volcano rabbits    A B C D

chimpanzees    A B C D

A = Their habitat's polluted.    C = People are moving into their habitat.
B = People are killing them.    D = People are destroying their habitat.

**1 A:** _____ are Komodo dragons endangered?

   **B:** They're endangered _____ _____ .

**2 A:** _____ are Andean flamingos endangered?

   **B:** They're endangered _____ _____ .

**3 A:** _____ are volcano rabbits endangered?

   **B:** They're endangered _____ _____ .

**4 A:** _____ are chimpanzees endangered?

   **B:** They're endangered _____ _____ .

**9** Write the question and answer.

_____

_____ (coconut crabs)?

_____

_____ (people destroying their habitat).

**10** **Read and choose the correct answers.**

1 A _______ hunts and kills animals to eat.

a predator    b trap

2 When there are only a few of one type of animal, they're _______.

a extinct    b endangered

3 People hunt red pandas for their _______.

a fur    b hair

4 Animals are not safe from diseases or hunting when they live in _______.

a the world    b the wild

92

**11** **Listen, read, and complete. Which animals do people keep as pets?**

bamboo    bumblebee    pandas    predators    salamander    tortoise    wild

## Status: Endangered

1 You can sometimes find [1]_______________ bats in caves in the forests of Myanmar and Thailand. However, there are now fewer than 6,000 left in the [2]_______________ because farmers burn the trees where they live.

2 Most red [3]_______________ live in China and the Himalayas, and they eat leaves. They hide in trees covered in red moss so that [4]_______________ don't see their beautiful red fur. They're endangered – there are now fewer than 10,000 – because people are destroying the [5]_______________ forests.

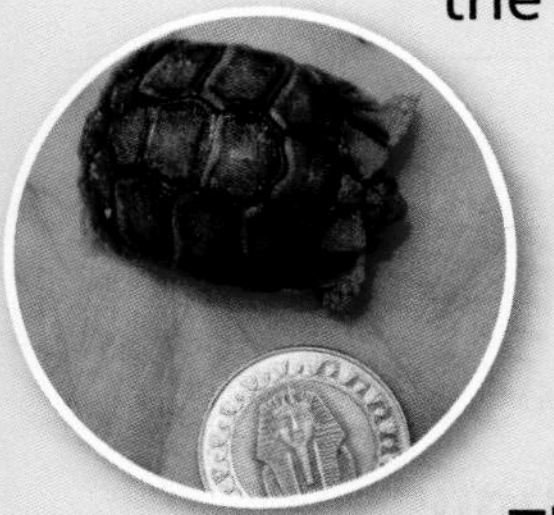

3 The Egyptian [6]_______________ is very small – it's only 10 centimeters long. That makes it the smallest of its kind in the world. Many scientists believe there are only 7,500 left in the wild now because people keep them as pets.

4 The Mexican walking fish lives on land and in water. It's called a fish, but it's really a type of [7]_______________, with small legs. Unfortunately, this strange fish is almost extinct. It lives in streams and ponds, but now its habitats are mostly polluted.

**12** Why is each animal endangered? Look at **11**. Then write the names and match.

1    2    3    4

_____    _____    _____    _____

a    b    c    d

**13** Complete the sentences.

> caves    extinct    polluted    pond    Scientists

**1** Bumbleebee bats live in _____ because they like the dark.

**2** The Mexican walking fish is nearly _____. There are fewer than 1,000 left.

**3** Rivers in towns and cities are often _____. You can't swim in them.

**4** _____ try to protect endangered species.

**5** There is a large _____ at the end of our yard with small fish and frogs.

**THINK BIG**

Which of these animals are extinct? Circle.

**1**   tiger / chimpanzee / giant panda / dodo

**2**   Asian elephant / mountain gorilla / T. rex / blue whale

**3**   orangutan / bumblebee bat / woolly mammoth / red panda

In what order did these three animals become extinct?

First: _____    Second: _____    Third: _____

**14** **Circle.**

1  We **could / couldn't** swim in the ocean because there were sharks.

2  Sara had a toothache, so she **could / couldn't** eat any cake.

3  Katie spoke French, so she **could / couldn't** understand everybody in Paris.

4  It rained, and we **could / couldn't** have our picnic.

5  Last year, students **could / couldn't** wear jeans. It was allowed.

6  In the morning, tourists **could / couldn't** visit the zoo. It was open.

**15** **Complete the questions about 14. Then write short answers.**

1  _____ (swim/they) in the ocean?  _____

2  _____ (eat/Sara) cake?  _____

3  _____ (speak/Katie) French?  _____

4  _____ (have/they) their picnic?  _____

5  _____ (when/wear/students) jeans?  _____

6  _____ (when/visit/tourists) the zoo?  _____

**16** **Look and write.**

| Fifty years ago, people... | ✓ | ✗ |
|---|---|---|
| the River Thames | swim in | go fishing in |
| Siberia | hunt tigers in | see many Amur tigers |
| Mexico City | find walking fish in ponds outside | visit the Mayan pyramids |

1  Fifty years ago, people _could swim in the River Thames, but they couldn't_
_____.

2  Fifty years ago, _____
_____.

3  _____
_____.

# Grammar

**17** **Circle the correct question words.**

1 **What / Where** do red pandas live?

2 **Why / Where** are Egyptian tortoises endangered?

3 **What / When** can you see bumblebee bats?

4 **Who / What** believes there are fewer than 10,000 red pandas?

5 **Where / What** is happening to forests in Thailand?

**18** **Look at 17. Match the answers to the questions.**

a People are cutting down the trees. ☐

b Scientists. ☐

c In bamboo forests. ☐

d Because they are popular pets. ☐

e At night or in the dark. ☐

**19** **Find and write questions. Use the words from the box.**

> What    Where    Who    Why

1 animals/be/endangered/in your country?

_____

2 be/your best friend/at school?

_____

3 go/you/on weekends?

_____

4 learn/you/English?

_____

**20** **Look at 19. Write answers for you.**

1 In my country, the gray wolf is endangered._____

2 _____

3 _____

4 _____

**21** **Read and complete.**

> breathe   giants   lizard   mythical   myths   real   scary   wings

There's only one ¹_____ dragon. It's the Komodo dragon, and it lives on a tiny Indonesian island. Actually, it isn't a dragon, it's a very large ²_____. All other dragons are ³_____ creatures. That means they exist only in ⁴_____ or fairy stories.

Some dragon tales are very frightening – they tell us about ⁵_____ beasts. These beasts are very large – they're ⁶_____ of the sky. They have enormous ⁷_____, and they ⁸_____ fire.

**22** **Listen, read, and circle.**

**1** In North America and Europe, dragons are
- **good** / **evil**
- **fire breathing** / **real**
- **funny** / **scary**

**2** In China, Japan, and Korea, dragons are
- beautiful and **magical** / **evil**
- **fire breathing** / **helpful**
- **scary** / **not scary**

**3** In Oceania and Australia, one dragon is
- called a **Western** / **bunyip**
- **friendly** / **scary**
- made of different parts of different **animals** / **people**

**4** In Indonesia, dragons are
- **real** / **mythical**
- **large lizards** / **birds**
- **extinct** / **endangered**

**23** Look at **21** and **22**. Read and circle **T** for true and **F** for false.

| | | | |
|---|---|---|---|
| **1** | Dragons are not mythical creatures. | T | F |
| **2** | All dragons can fly. | T | F |
| **3** | In North America and Europe, dragons are evil. | T | F |
| **4** | Dragons in China are made up of different animal parts. | T | F |
| **5** | In Oceania, dragons are scary. | T | F |
| **6** | Dragons are extinct in Indonesia. | T | F |
| **7** | In Japan, dragons are lucky. | T | F |
| **8** | In Indonesia, dragons are large lizards. | T | F |

**24** Find and write four pairs of synonyms and three pairs of antonyms.

**1** tale

**a** story

**2** giant

**b** frightening

**3** humans

**c** evil

**4** good

**d** south

**5** scary

**e** mythical

**6** real

**f** people

**7** north

**g** very big

| Synonyms | Antonyms |
|---|---|
| | |
| | |
| | |
| | |

**THINK BIG** Where can you see examples of dragons or mythical creatures? Think of five places.

1 _____   2 _____   3 _____

4 _____   5 _____

**25** **Look and match.**

1 exclamation point
2 period
3 question mark

**26** **Put a period, a question mark, or an exclamation point.**

1 How many chimps were there 100 years ago____

2 Coconut crabs live on islands in the Pacific Ocean____

3 Wow____ That frog is so amazing____

4 Why are chimps endangered____

5 Look____ A dragon____

6 They have a population of 100,000____

**27** **Write sentences. Use a period, a question mark, or an exclamation point.**

1

angler fish

_____

_____

2

tigers

_____

_____

3

Tasmanian devils

_____

_____

4

volcano rabbits

_____

_____

5

Andean condors

_____

_____

6
black rhinos

_____

_____

**28** **Read and circle ph and wh.**

phone    panda    wheel

phantom

photo    white    wild

whale    wheat

dolphin    fish

**29** **Underline the words with ph and wh. Then read aloud.**

**1**  When was the white elephant in the wheat?

**2**  I took a photo with my phone of a whale and a dolphin.

**30** **Connect the letters. Then write.**

**1**  ph                          en        **a** _ _ _ _

**2**  wh                         one       **b** _ _ _ _ _

**31** **Listen and write.**

The phantom has a ¹_____

On his ²_____

Of a ³_____ wheel

And some ⁴_____ .

**32** **Unscramble and complete.**

**1** Some scientists believe there are fewer than 7,500 Egyptian tortoises left in the _____. (ldiw)

**2** Most bumblebee bats live in _____ in Thailand. (vesac)

**3** Red pandas eat _____ leaves. (ooambb)

**4** Most scientists believe that the Mexican walking fish is almost _____. (cnetxit)

**33** **Complete the dialogs with words from the box.**

| because | chimpanzees | habitat | how many |
|---------|-------------|---------|----------|
| tarsiers | there are | there were | |

**1**

**A:** Why are _____ endangered?

**B:** They're endangered _____ people are destroying their _____.

**2**

**A:** _____ Andean condors are there now?

**B:** _____ only about 10,000 left in the wild.

**3**

**A:** How many _____ were there a hundred years ago?

**B:** _____ more than a million.

**34** **Read and write could or couldn't.**

**A:** We ¹_____ touch the Komodo dragons. They're too dangerous. People ²_____ only look at them from far away.

**B:** ³_____ you watch them eat?

**A:** Yes. They ⁴_____ fit a small deer in their mouth! It was amazing!

# Life Long Ago

**1** **Read and write the letters. Then trace the path.**

**L** travel by car

**I** traveled by horse and buggy

**G** had oil lamps

**E** listened to the radio

**N** cook in a microwave

**O** washed clothes by hand

**L** wash clothes in a washing machine

**G** cooked on a coal stove

**A** have electric lights

**F** listen to an MP3 player

**O** have a cell phone

**!** used a phone with an operator

**2** **Look at the letters in 1. Follow the path and write the letters. What do they spell?**

\_\_\_\_ \_\_\_\_ \_\_\_\_ \_\_\_\_ \_\_\_\_ - \_\_\_\_ \_\_\_\_ \_\_\_\_ \_\_\_\_ \_\_\_\_ \_\_\_\_ - \_\_\_\_ \_\_\_\_ \_\_\_\_ \_\_\_\_ \_\_\_\_ \_\_\_\_

## 3 Listen and match.

### In the Old Days

**a**

Now there's water from the tap.

**c**

Now there are computers.

**e**

Now a lot of people have cars.

Life one hundred years ago
Was different, you see.
¹There were no computers,
²And there was no TV.

**Life was different in the old days.
Life was different in so many ways.**

³Children used to get water
From pumps or wells outdoors.
Now we just turn on the tap,
And out fresh water pours!

**Chorus**

Life was so much slower!
⁴Few people had a car.
⁵Children used to walk to school,
And they walked very far!

**Chorus**

**b**

Now there's TV.

**d**

Now kids take a school bus.

## 4 Write about now and long ago.

Now

Long Ago

_____   _____
_____   _____
_____   _____
_____   _____
_____   _____
_____   _____

**5** **Read. Then circle T for true and F for false.**

Life was Nicer Then

Sam and his grandma are watching the TV. Sam wants to change the channel, but he's too lazy to get the TV remote control. They didn't have remote controls when Sam's grandma was a child. They used to walk to the TV to change the channel. They only had three channels when Grandma was young, and she thinks life was nicer then.

The microwave beeps. Grandma sometimes uses a microwave to make dinner. Maybe some things about modern life are nicer!

**1** Grandma is too lazy to change the channel.     **T     F**

**2** People didn't watch TV when Sam's grandma was young.     **T     F**

**3** There were no remote controls when Sam's grandma was a child.     **T     F**

**4** There are only three channels now.     **T     F**

**5** Grandma uses a microwave to cook.     **T     F**

**THINK BIG**

**What did your grandma have when she was a child? Read and ✓ or ✗. Then write.**

computer ☐   phone ☐   washing machine ☐   microwave ☐
car ☐   bike ☐   TV remote control ☐   books ☐   radio ☐

My grandma had _____

_____.

She didn't have _____

_____.

### 6 Listen and stick. Number in order.

109

a  ☐

b  ☐

c  ☐

d  ☐

### 7 Read and write the answers. Use **did** or **didn't**.

**1 A:** Did your grandma have a
TV when she was young?

**B:** _____

**2 A:** Did people have cars fifty
years ago?

**B:** _____

**3 A:** Did your grandad play video
games when he was a child?

**B:** _____

**4 A:** Did people have washing
machines 200 hundred years ago?

**B:** _____

### 8 Complete the questions and answers.

**1**

**A:** _____ mom _____
a cell phone at school?

**B:** _____, _____.
She used public phones.

**2**

**A:** _____ dad _____
a computer at school?

**B:** _____, _____.
It was big and slow.

**9** **Complete the sentences.**

**1** **A:** Before computers, how _____ keep in touch?

**B:** They _____.

**2** **A:** Before washing machines, how _____ wash clothes?

**B:** They _____.

**3** **A:** Before electricity, what _____ for light?

**B:** They _____.

**4** **A:** Before cars, what _____ for transportation?

**B:** They _____.

**10** **Answer about you.**

**1** When she was young, what did your grandma use to do at night?

_____

**2** When you were six, how did you use to go to school?

_____

**11** **Look in your house. What used to be different?**

**1** _____

_____

**2** _____

_____

**3** _____

_____

**12** **Complete the sentences.**

| average speed | distance | engine | multiply | number of | per hour |

**1** The _____ of a modern plane is about 885 km per hour.

**2** Planes are a great way to travel a long _____ because they're fast.

**3** The average man can walk at a speed of 5 km _____.

**4** Bad traffic means there is a large _____ cars on the roads.

**5** If you _____ ten by ten, it makes a hundred.

**6** A car can't travel without an _____.

**13** **Listen, read, and circle. How did people travel before cars?**

1    What did people do before they had cars? Well, lucky people used to travel by horse and buggy. And unlucky people walked. Both forms of travel were **¹uncomfortable / slow**, but the horse and buggy was a little more comfortable. It had an average speed of 8 kilometers (km) per hour. Historians believe people didn't travel for longer than about three hours per day, probably because it was very **²tiring / expensive**.

Horse and Buggy

Model T

2    Mr. Henry Ford built the first Model T, or "Tin Lizzie," in 1908. It changed the way we travel. For the first time, a car was not a luxury. The car became a **³popular / cheap** means of transport, and everybody with a job and some money could buy one. The Model T had an average speed of 40 km per hour. Suddenly, there were more vehicles on the roads, and it was more **⁴exciting / dangerous**.

3    Today, there are many different **⁵modern / new** cars. Some are for racing, some are luxury cars, and some are family cars. They're all faster than they used to be. An average family car can travel at a speed of more than 150 km per hour. But they never do. The average speed of modern cars is 90 km per hour. This is because there are strict speed limits, and there is a lot of **⁶noise / traffic**.

Modern Car

**14** **Look at 13. Read and answer.**

**1** How many hours did people travel each day with a horse and buggy?

_____

**2** Who could buy a Model T? _____

**3** Today, cars can't travel fast. Why not?

_____

**15** **Look at the average speeds in 13 and solve the equations.**

**1** A horse and buggy travels for 10 hours. How far does it travel?

_____ x _____ = _____ km
average    number    distance
speed    of hours    traveled

**2** A Model T travels for 6 hours. How far does it travel?

_____ x _____ = _____ km

**3** A horse and buggy travels for 8 hours. How far does it travel?

_____ x _____ = _____ km

**4** A modern car travels for 2 hours. How far does it travel?

_____ x _____ = _____ km

**5** A Model T travels for 7 hours. How far does it travel?

_____ x _____ = _____ km

**6** A modern car travels for 3 hours. How far does it travel?

_____ x _____ = _____ km

**THINK BIG**

**Look at 15 and cross out the answers. Then use the other numbers to make a new equation.**

| 3 | 40 | 64 | 80 | 120 | 180 | 240 | 270 | 280 |

A Model T travels for _____ hours. How far does it travel?

_____ x _____ = _____ km

**16** **What were these people doing yesterday? Complete.**

1 At 8 o'clock, the Graham family _____were swimming_____ (swim) in a lake.

2 At 9 o'clock, Mrs. Cross _____ (put) clothes in her washing machine.

3 At 10 o'clock, Harry's dog _____ (eat) an old shoe.

4 At 11 o'clock, Jordan's sister _____ (look) out of the car window. She _____ (feel) very bored.

5 At 12 o'clock, the Gray twins _____ (watch) their favorite DVD.

6 At 2 o'clock, the next-door neighbors _____ (have) a barbecue in their backyard.

**17** **Look and write.**

1 8 a.m. – Dad
wait for the bus ✓
drive ✗

_At 8 a.m., Dad was waiting for the bus. He wasn't driving._

2 12 a.m. – dog
bark loudly ✗
go for a walk ✓

_____

3 6 p.m. – Mom
cook dinner ✗
have pizza with friends ✓

_____

4 7 p.m. – Eli
play computer games ✓
do homework ✗

_____

5 8 p.m. – Sofia
watch TV ✗
study ✓

_____

6 11 a.m. – Dad
sleep ✗
run ✓

_____

# Grammar

**18** **Write questions.**

**1** what/you/do/at 10 p.m./last night ?

_____

**2** you/watch TV/at 8 a.m./yesterday morning ?

_____

**3** you/have/breakfast/at 9 a.m. ?

_____

**4** where/you/go/after school/yesterday afternoon ?

_____

**5** your family/eat/dinner/at 8 p.m./last night ?

_____

**19** **Look at 18. Answer the questions for you.**

**1** _____

**2** _____

**3** _____

**4** _____

**5** _____

**20** **Complete the sentences.**

> had    only goes    used to go    was feeling    was racing
> was traveling    were driving    were enjoying

When Carlos was young, he ¹_____ on vacation with his family every year. Now he ²_____ with his friends! One August, they ³_____ through France for their summer vacation. Dad ⁴_____ a brand-new car. Carlos's parents ⁵_____ themselves, but Carlos ⁶_____ bored. The car ⁷_____ at an average speed of 90 km per hour – so fast that Carlos couldn't see anything. Carlos asked for a bike.

That summer, Carlos's parents drove, and Carlos cycled. Five years later, Carlos ⁸_____ his bicycle in the Tour de France competition!

**21** **Read and circle.**

1 When you don't have **technology** / **running water**, it's difficult to keep the house clean.

2 Your **tribe** / **nomad** is the people you live with. A tribe is like a big family.

3 If your house doesn't have **heat** / **electricity**, you can't use a computer or a TV.

4 **Traditional** / **cultural** habits are old habits from the past.

5 Cell phones, computers, and TVs all use modern **electricity** / **technology**.

**22** **Listen, read, and write. Which tribe changes home quite often?**

| ancestors forests language nomadic reindeer tundra |

### The Hmong

1     The Hmong are hill people. They live in the mountains of Southeast Asia. They have their own way of life and their own ¹_____. You won't find much modern technology in a traditional Hmong village because people there live the way their ²_____ did 2,000 years ago.

### The Maasai

2     The Maasai of Kenya are a ³_____ tribe. This means they move from place to place and make new homes each time. They often live in ⁴_____ and build their homes out of things they can find in nature. Their villages don't have running water or electricity, so they can't use modern technology in their homes.

### The Koryak

3     The Koryak live in the northern part of Russia's Pacific coast. Their land is Arctic ⁵_____, and it's very cold. For food, they herd ⁶_____ and catch fish. Koryak children don't have time for playing computer games or surfing the Internet because they hunt for their food with their parents. They also make some of their clothes. They wear warm hats made of reindeer skins to protect them from the freezing temperatures.

**23** **Look at 22 and ✓.**

|   | The Hmong | The Koryak | The Maasai |
|---|---|---|---|
| **1** live in Russia. | | | |
| **2** move from place to place. | | | |
| **3** live in Southeast Asia. | | | |
| **4** wear reindeer skin hats. | | | |
| **5** live in Kenya. | | | |
| **6** live like people did 2,000 years ago. | | | |

**24** **Look at 22. Choose words from the box to match the definitions.**

**1** These are people from your family or tribe who aren't alive. _____

**2** We use this to speak and communicate. _____

**3** These people don't stay in one place. _____

**4** It's a dry and cold place, and there aren't many trees. _____

**5** This is a large animal that likes cold weather. _____

**Which of these things are most difficult?
Number 1 (not very difficult) to 5 (very difficult).**

THINK
BIG

**building your own house** ☐

**moving every few years** ☐

**looking for water to drink** ☐

**living in the mountains** ☐

**living without electricity** ☐

**looking for food** ☐

**living in a very cold place** ☐

**Which tribe do you think lives the most difficult life? Why?**

_____

_____

**25** **Put quotation marks in the correct places.**

1 Did they watch movies in the 1920s? he asked.
2 I used to play soccer, said John.
3 Jamie yelled, I got a new bike!
4 Karen said, I wrote a letter last night.

**26** **Rewrite the sentences. Use said or asked and quotation marks.**

How did people travel in 1905?

Did you use to ride in a horse and buggy?

They used to ride in a horse and buggy.

I'm not that old!

Ed     Mom

1 _____

2 _____

3 _____

4 _____

**27** **Look and write what they are saying. Use said, asked, or yelled and quotation marks.**

_____          _____

1

2

**28** **Read and circle ge and dge.**

fridge    cage    watched

traditional    washed    large

badge    edge

bridge    page    age

**29** **Underline the words with ge and dge. Then read aloud.**

**1** Look over the edge of the hedge. There's a bridge.

**2** The boy's wearing a large badge and carrying a cage.

**30** **Connect the letters. Then write.**

| | | | |
|---|---|---|---|
| **1** ca | dge | **a** _ _ _ _ |
| **2** ba | ge | **b** _ _ _ _ _ |
| **3** lar | ge | **c** _ _ _ _ |
| **4** e | dge | **d** _ _ _ _ _ |

**31** **Listen and write.**

There's a $^1$ _____ fridge

On the $^2$ _____ .

There's a large $^3$ _____

In the $^4$ _____ .

**32** **Read and solve the equations.**

**1** A school bus has an average speed of 60 kilometers per hour. How far does it travel in 3 hours?

_____ x _____ = _____ km

**2** A bike has an average speed of 20 kilometers per hour. How far does it travel in 6 hours?

_____ x _____ = _____ km

**33** **Circle and write.**

**1** **A: Did / Do** people have microwaves 100 years ago?

**B:** _____

**2** **A:** Did your city or town **had / have** cars ten years ago?

**B:** _____

**3** **A:** Did people **use to / used to** listen to MP3 players before electricity?

**B:** _____

**4** **A:** Did your dad **travel / traveled** to school by horse and buggy?

**B:** _____

**34** **Circle four things that didn't exist long ago. Write sentences with didn't use to in your notebook.**

**35** **What were you and you family doing at these times yesterday?**

8 o' clock in the morning _____

12 o' clock, lunchtime _____

7 o' clock in the evening _____

# Sue's Path

**1** Look at Units 4, 5, and 6. Choose words from the units. Write them in the charts.

**2** Draw one path. Gather information and add your own.

**HEALTH PROBLEMS**

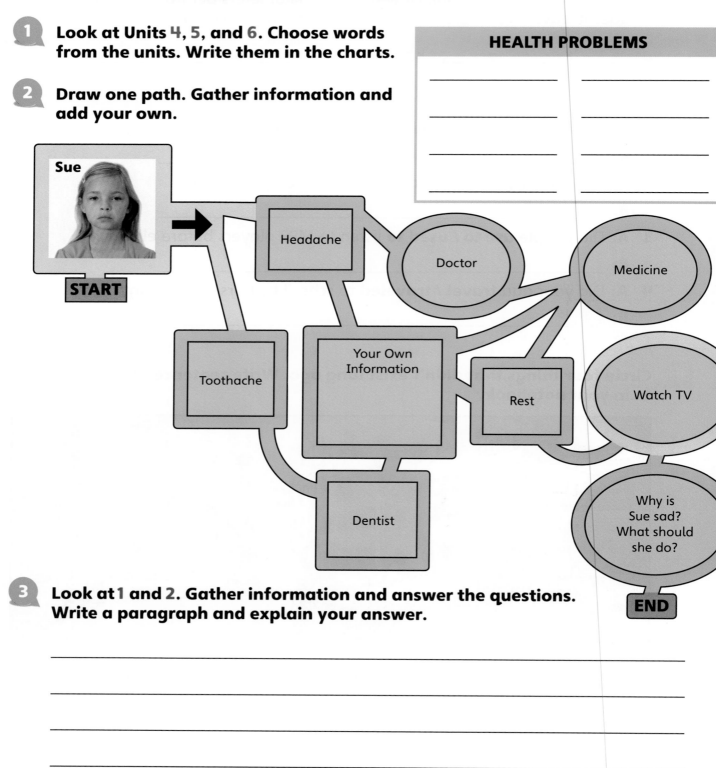

**3** Look at 1 and 2. Gather information and answer the questions. Write a paragraph and explain your answer.

## ENDANGERED ANIMALS

_____

_____

_____

_____

## TECHNOLOGY NOW

_____

_____

_____

**END**

Endangered Animals

TIGERS:
Used to be
100,000.
Fewer than
3,200!

KOMODO
DRAGON:
Used to be
20,000.
Fewer than
5,000!

Why
are they
endangered?
What should
we do?

**END**

Long Ago
and Now

Your Own
Information

What did
people use?
What do they
use now?

**unit 7**

# Special Days

**1** **Look and write the special days.**

1 _____

2 _____

3 _____

4 _____

5 _____

6 _____

**2** **Read and circle T for true and F for false.**

1 My parents' anniversary is celebrated by my mom and dad.    **T**    **F**

2 New Year's Day is before New Year's Eve.    **T**    **F**

3 School Sports Day is for parents, not kids.    **T**    **F**

4 My dad celebrates Father's Day.    **T**    **F**

**3**  **Listen and write. Use the words from the box.**

## What Do We Do on Special Days?

This ¹_____ is a special day —
   The last day of the year.
We're ²_____ stay up very late.
   At midnight, we're going to cheer!

**Special days are cool. Special days are fun.**
**Special days bring special treats for everyone!**

On the first of ³_____,
   We are going to say,
   "Happy New Year!" to everyone
Because it's ⁴_____.

### Chorus

There are a lot of special days,
   And this one is a treat.
   We're going to
Have ⁵_____
And ⁶_____,
And delicious food to eat!

### Chorus

| fireworks |
| Friday |
| going to |
| January |
| New Year's Day |
| parades |

---

**4** **Look at 3 and ✓ the correct answers.**

**1** This Friday is…

☐ December 30th.   ☐ December 31st.   ☐ January 1st.

**2** They are going to cheer…

☐ at lunchtime.   ☐ in the afternoon.   ☐ at midnight.

**3** On New Year's Eve, they…

☐ stay up late.   ☐ go to bed early.   ☐ sleep late.

**5** **Read. Then answer the questions.**

### The Anniversary Party

Sam knows his parents' wedding anniversary is the 10th. He's planning a big celebration for their anniversary on June 10th. They're going to go out for a special dinner. Sam is making a cake. His parents like the plans, but there's a problem. Their anniversary is on July 10th, not June 10th!

**1** Why is Sam planning a celebration? _____

**2** Where are they going to go? _____

**3** What's the problem? _____

**6** **Write about you and your family.**

**1** My birthday is on _____.

**2** My mom's birthday is on _____.

**3** My dad's birthday is on _____.

**4** My parents' wedding anniversary is on _____.

**Think and write. What do you think Sam's parents are going to say next?**

THINK BIG

_____
_____

_____
_____

**7** Listen and stick. Then listen and write the special day and what they are going to do.

1

2

3

_____

_____

_____

_____

_____

_____

**8** Answer the questions about Sarah's calendar.

| Sun | Mon | Tue | Wed | Thu | Fri | Sat |
|-----|-----|-----|-----|-----|-----|-----|
| 1 | 2 | 3 Today | 4 | 5 | 6 | 7 Birthday party |
| 8 | 9 | 10 | 11 Parents' anniversary | 12 | 13 | 14 Sister visits friend |
| 15 | 16 | 17 | 18 Watch parade | 19 | 20 | 21 Watch fireworks |

**1** When is Sarah going to have her birthday party? _____

_____

**2** When are her parents going to celebrate their anniversary? _____

_____

**3** When is her sister going to visit her friend? _____

_____

**4** Is she going to watch the parade on the 17th? _____

**5** Are they going to watch the fireworks on Saturday? _____

**9** **Listen and match.**

| Mom's birthday | | sports day | | Father's Day |
|---|---|---|---|---|

<table>
<tr><th colspan="7">JUNE</th></tr>
<tr><th>SUNDAY</th><th>MONDAY</th><th>TUESDAY</th><th>WEDNESDAY</th><th>THURSDAY</th><th>FRIDAY</th><th>SATURDAY</th></tr>
<tr><td></td><td></td><td></td><td></td><td></td><td>1</td><td>2</td></tr>
<tr><td>3</td><td>4</td><td>5</td><td>6</td><td>7</td><td>8</td><td>9</td></tr>
<tr><td>10</td><td>11</td><td>12</td><td>13</td><td>14</td><td>15</td><td>16</td></tr>
<tr><td>17</td><td>18</td><td>19</td><td>20</td><td>21</td><td>22</td><td>23</td></tr>
<tr><td>24</td><td>25</td><td>26</td><td>27</td><td>28</td><td>29</td><td>30</td></tr>
</table>

watch a parade

Grandparents' anniversary

Midsummer's Day

**10** **Read and cross out the letters. Then write the special days.**

**1** Cross out the first, third, fifth, ninth, tenth, twelfth, and fourteenth letters.

G E T A B R T H L N D O A M Y

— — — — —    — — —

**2** Cross out the first, third, seventh, tenth, thirteenth, sixteenth, seventeenth, and twentieth letters.

B M O I D S R U M H M E P R S Y N D A O Y

— — — — — — — — ' — — — — —

**3** Cross out the second, fourth, sixth, seventh, ninth, eleventh, sixteenth, seventeenth, and nineteenth letters.

N A E H W P V Y I E N A R S D E V A E Y

— — — — — — — ' — — — —

**11** **Complete the sentences.**

> attraction    clean    fight    takes place    torches

**1** Every year in Buñol, there is a big tomato _____.  ☐

**2** In one festival in Thailand, people carry fire _____ down from the mountain.  ☐

**3** The Monkey Buffet festival in Thailand isn't a popular tourist _____.  ☐

**4** It's very unusual to leave the Holi festival wearing _____ clothes.  ☐

**5** Quyllur Rit'i _____ only in June.  ☐

**12** **Listen, read, and circle. Are the sentences in 11 correct? Put a ✓ or a ✗.**

### Holi, The Festival of Colors

1     This festival takes place every year to **¹watch / celebrate** the end of winter and the arrival of spring. It's celebrated in India, Nepal, and other places. It's probably the most colorful festival in the whole world. During Holi, people throw water and colored **²paper / powder**. People like to wear white clothes to Holi and watch them stain with all the different colors.

### Tomatina, The Tomato Festival

2     Every year, on the last Wednesday of August, there is a **³clean / messy** festival in Buñol, Spain, where people throw tomatoes at each other. The festival started in 1945. There was no real reason for it. It was just good fun.

### The Monkey Buffet

3     On the last weekend in November, the people of Lopburi, Thailand, invite hundreds of monkeys to a **⁴feast / fight** of peanuts, fruit, and vegetables. People come from all over the world to watch the monkeys eat.

### Quyllur Rit'i , The Festival of the Snow Star

4     It takes place every year in May or June on a **⁵volcano / glacier** in Peru. People celebrate with music and dancing for three days and nights, and the festival finishes with everyone carrying fire torches as they leave.

**13** Look at 12. Circle **T** for true and **F** for false.

1 The Festival of Colors takes place in China.    T    F

2 People usually wear white clothes to Holi.    T    F

3 The Tomato Festival is celebrated in Spain.    T    F

4 People celebrate it to say "thank you" for all the tomatoes.    T    F

5 The Monkey Buffet takes place at the end of November
in Thailand.    T    F

6 People celebrate the Festival of the Snow Star for three
weeks in Peru.    T    F

**14** Answer the questions.

1 Who are the guests at the Monkey Buffet?

_____

2 What makes the streets messy at the Tomato Festival?

_____

3 Why is it icy cold at the Festival of the Snow Star?

_____

4 Why does the colored powder stick to clothes at Holi?

_____

**Think and write. What are you going to take with you?**

THINK
BIG    You're going to the Tomato Festival.

_____

You're going to the Festival of the Snow Star.

_____

**15** **Read and choose the correct answers.**

**1** Sara _____ a new dress yesterday because she's going to a wedding on Saturday.

   **a** bought          **b** is buying

**2** Damian took his violin to school because he _____ in the school concert later.

   **a** played          **b** is going to play

**3** We watched a program about animals in the wild because we _____ a project next week at school.

   **a** did             **b** are doing

**4** Mom _____ Dad a cake this afternoon because it's his fortieth birthday tomorrow.

   **a** baking          **b** baked

**5** Dad _____ some more gas in the car last night because we're going on a long trip.

   **a** puts            **b** put

**6** I gave my old cell phone to my little sister because I'm _____ a new one!

   **a** going to get     **b** get

**16** **Complete the sentences. Use the correct form of the verb.**

**1** Tim _____ (not study) last night because he's going to study today.

**2** Gail wasn't at the party because she _____ (go) on vacation with her family tomorrow.

**3** Marie _____ (not meet) her friend yesterday because she was busy.

**4** They woke up very early because they're _____ (climb) a mountain today.

**5** We didn't bring our swimming suits because we _____ (not swim) today.

**6** I finished my chores quickly today because I _____ (watch) a DVD with my best friend later.

# Grammar

**17** **Match. Then write sentences. Use going to.**

1 Dad/buy/a new camera

2 We/decorate/our classroom

3 Mom/buy/gifts

4 Kim/learn/all about computers

**because**

5 Tom/stay/at home

6 Jenny/eat/a big dinner

a run in a race tomorrow.

b take pictures of the Monkey Buffet.

c get a new laptop.

d watch his favorite TV program.

e meet our American cousins.

f have visitors from a school abroad.

1 _____

2 _____

3 _____

4 _____

5 _____

6 _____

**18** **Complete the sentences for you.**

1 _____ because I'm going to meet a friend after school this afternoon.

2 I went to bed early because _____.

3 My mom bought me some new clothes _____.

4 _____ because I'm going to go on vacation with my friend's family.

**19** **Read and choose the correct answers.**

**1** What don't you see on a calendar?

   **a** dates    **b** numbers    **c** days    **d** planets

**2** Which one is a superstition?

   **a** I usually eat chicken on Mondays.

   **b** I always buy birthday gifts for friends.

   **c** I wouldn't marry in a leap year.

**3** When you propose, you usually…

   **a** invite someone to your party.

   **b** borrow some money.

   **c** ask someone to marry you.

139

**20** **Listen, read, and write the numbers. Which day is the leap day?**

> 49    366    2008    1    29    365

**1**    We usually say a year is ¹_____ days long because that's about the time it takes Earth to travel around the Sun. It actually takes 365 days, 5 hours, ²_____ minutes, and 12 seconds. The extra 5 hours, 49 minutes, and 12 seconds add up to an extra day every four years – on February ³_____th. This day is called leap day. Years with the extra day are called leap years. These years always have ⁴_____ days. We know when there's a leap year because these years can be divided evenly by four. For example, 2004, ⁵_____, and 2012 were leap years.

**2**    The leap year was put on the calendar only in the ⁶_____st century BC. In ancient times, people were very superstitious about them.

**3**    In modern times, it's a tradition in many countries for women to propose to their boyfriends on a leap day. Traditionally, men propose to women. But not on leap days! On a leap day, if the woman proposes but the man says "no," he must buy the woman a gift.

**4**    The only really unlucky people are the ones with birthdays on February 29th. This means their birthday comes only once every four years!

**21** **Look at 20. Answer the questions.**

**1** How long does it take Earth to travel around the Sun?

_____ days

_____ hours

_____ minutes

_____ seconds

**2** How many days are there in a leap year? _____

**22** **Solve these problems.**

**1** Billy was born on February 29th, 2000. Write the next four years he can celebrate his birthday on February 29th.

_____    _____    _____    _____

**2** It's February 29th, 2012. It's Jessi's birthday. Write the next four years she can celebrate her birthday on February 29th.

_____    _____    _____    _____

**23** **Read and complete.**

Greece    leap years    unlucky

Julius Caesar created [1]_____ in the 1st century BC. Greeks and Romans were very superstitious about this year. They thought it was [2]_____ to start a journey, start a new job, marry, or buy or sell something in a leap year. In [3]_____, some people still think it's very unlucky to marry in a leap year.

THINK BIG

**What do people believe about leap years in your country? Do they think leap years are good or bad?**

_____

**What's a common superstition in your country?**

_____

**24** **Look and complete the email. Use the words from the box.**

FROM ¹ _____

TO  alex@bigenglish.com

SUBJECT ² _____

³ _____ Alex,

Guess what! It's our street carnival next weekend. There are loads of things planned. I'm going to watch the parade because my sister's in it. She's going to wear special traditional clothes. Then I'm going to buy a present for my grandparents. It's their anniversary on June 13th.

I have to go. Write back soon!

⁴ _____

Simon

Dear
Next weekend
simon@bigenglish.com
Your friend,

**25** **Write an email to a friend. Invite your friend to a celebration.**

New Year's Day party    Midsummer's Day party

FROM

TO

SUBJECT

**26** **Read and circle ue, e_e, and ure.**

cute

glue

bridge

sponge

edge

picture

blue

cube

true

treasure

**27** **Underline the words with ue, u_e, and ure. Then read aloud.**

**1** This is a huge bottle of glue.

**2** I drink pure water.

**28** **Connect the letters. Then write.**

**1** bl

**2** c

**3** nat

ure

ue

ube

**a** _ _ _ _ _ _

**b** _ _ _ _

**c** _ _ _ _

144
**29** **Listen and write.**

Hi, ¹ _____.

Is it ² _____?

It's so ³ _____.

It's so ⁴ _____.

It's really ⁵ _____!

Is that a monster

In the ⁶ _____?

**30  Read and answer.**

Sam's going to the dentist on the ninth of March. On the fifteenth of March, he's going to visit his aunt and uncle. His cousins are on vacation, so on the twentieth of March, he's going to visit them. They're going to go to the movies together.

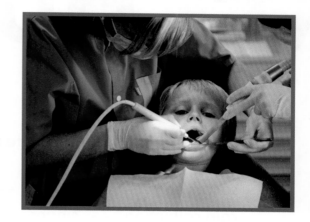

**1**  Where is Sam going on March 9th? _____

**2**  What is he going to do on March 15th? _____

**3**  Is he going to see his cousins on the 15th? _____

**4**  Is he going to see his cousins on the 20th? _____

**31  Read and match.**

**1**  give a                         **a**  clothes

**2**  have a                        **b**  a present

**3**  watch a                      **c**  parade

**4**  watch                         **d**  party

**5**  wear different           **e**  card

**6**  get                             **f**  fireworks

**32  Read and write. Use the words from the box.**

During    For    last    takes place

**1**  The Festival of Colors _____ every year in India.

**2**  _____ three days and nights, people celebrate with music.

**3**  The Tomato Festival is on the _____ Wednesday of August.

**4**  _____ the Monkey Buffet festival, monkeys feast on fruit and vegetables.

# Hobbies

**1** **Draw the path. Connect the pictures. Then complete the question and answer.**

soccer player  → painter → toy car collection → chess player →

coin collection → singer → video game player → shell collection →

doll collection → dancer → basketball player → writer

Y
I
E
H
S
S
O
B
H
R
S
Y
R
B
Y
Y
U
O
O
Y

What _____?

_____

## 2 Listen and circle. Then answer the questions.

### The Best and the Worst

Matthew collects toy cars.
He has one hundred seven.
But Pam's **car / shell** collection is
bigger.
She has three hundred
**eleven / ten**!

Kay is good at games.
She's really good at **music / chess**.
But Paul is even better than Kay.
And Liz, well, she's the best!

**What's your hobby, Bobby?**
**What do you like doing?**
**What's your hobby, Bobby?**
**What is fun for you?**

Steve's a **great / terrible** singer.
Emma's worse than Steve.
But David's singing is the worst.
When he sings, people leave!

It's **bad / good** to have a hobby.
Some people have a few.
Even if you're not the best,
It still is fun to do!

**Chorus**

**1** Who collects toy cars? _____

**2** How many cars does Matthew have? _____

**3** How many cars does Pam have? _____

**4** Who is the best at games? _____

**5** Is Steve a good singer? _____

**6** Do people like listening to David's singing? _____

**3** **Read. Then circle T for true and F for false.**

## The School Play

Christina's dad is excited about this year's school play. The play is *Snow White*. He wants Christina to be a star in the play. He wants her to be an important character, like Snow White or the Evil Queen. Christina didn't get either of those parts. Her friends Lizzie and Ruth got those parts because they're better singers and actors than Christina. But Christina's the tallest girl in the class, so she's going to be a tree. It's a small part, but Christina's dad is very proud of her.

| | | | |
|---|---|---|---|
| **1** | Christina's dad thinks the school play is boring. | **T** | **F** |
| **2** | He wants Christina to be Snow White. | **T** | **F** |
| **3** | Christina is a better singer than Lizzie. | **T** | **F** |
| **4** | Christina is taller than all the other girls. | **T** | **F** |
| **5** | Christina's going to be a tree. | **T** | **F** |

**4** **Write about you.**

**1** What character would you like to be in *Snow White*? Why?

_____

**2** What are you good at?

_____

**THINK BIG** **Think about Snow White and the Evil Queen. Who do you like better? Why? Use the words from the box.**

friendly
kind   nice
old   pretty

_____

**5** Listen and stick. Then number and write. Use the words from the box.

> the best   the coolest   the worst

a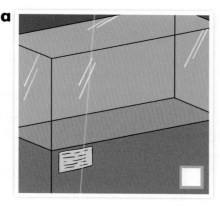

b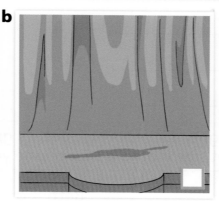

c

_____   _____   _____

**6** Complete the table. Use the words from the box.

> bad   better   the best   the worst

| | worse | | good | | |
|---|---|---|---|---|---|

**7** Read and circle the correct words. Then match.

1  Susan's team is **good** / **better** at basketball. ☐

2  Cassie's story is the **longer** / **longest** story. ☐

3  Grandpa used to be the **good** / **best** painter in the city. ☐

4  Diane is worse **than** / **of** Claire at video games. ☐

5  Jason has a **better** / **good** shell collection than Craig. ☐

6  This is the **oldest** / **older** doll in my collection. ☐

a

b

c

d

e

f

**8** **Read. Then use a form of big or old to complete each sentence.**

> Philip has two brothers and three sisters. Pablo has three brothers and four sisters. Tony has two brothers and two sisters.

**1** Philip's family is _____ Tony's.

**2** Pablo's family is _____ of all.

**3** Tony's family is _____.

> Dean's grandma is eighty-six years old. Betty's grandma is seventy-four years old. Harriet's grandma is ninety-one years old.

**4** Dean's grandma is _____ Betty's grandma.

**5** Betty's grandma is _____.

**6** Harriet's grandma is _____ of all.

**9** **Read and answer for you.**

**1** What are you good at?

_____

**2** What is your mom or dad good at?

_____

**3** What is your brother or sister good at?

_____

**4** What are you bad at?

_____

**5** What is your best friend bad at?

_____

**6** What is your cousin bad at?

_____

**10** **Number the pictures.**

> **1** butterfly collection   **2** doll   **3** embroidery   **4** soccer

**a**    **b**    **c**    **d**

156

**11** **Listen, read, and circle six mistakes. Then write the correct words.**

> china   drawing   employers   rocking   skirts   thread

1     Many sports today are not new. Soccer became popular in the 19th century. Back then, many soccer clubs were started by teachers so that the workers could play and stay fit. However, only male workers could play. Soccer was a man's sport. Both women and men played tennis and croquet. Sports for women were not easy because they had to wear long trousers.

**1** _____   **2** _____

2     Girls used to spend a lot of time at home. They did quiet activities with their hands. Many girls liked doing embroidery with a needle and rope. They used to embroider cushions and tablecloths. They also created beautiful pictures of flowers and birds with tiny colored stitches. **3**_____

3     In the 19th century, the choice of toys for girls and boys was much smaller. Girls used to play with dolls and dollhouses. They had to be careful because the dolls were made of plastic. They could break quite easily. Jumping horses were also popular with boys and girls. Boys used to play with toy trains and railways.

**4** _____   **5** _____

4     People in the 19th century loved nature. One popular hobby was collecting and playing with butterflies. They caught the butterflies in nets then pinned them on boards to show their beautiful colors. **6**_____

**12** **Look at 11. Read and circle.**

In the 19th century,

**1** many men played soccer **in the park / at work**.

**2** women used to play **with trains / croquet**.

**3** women **went out / stayed at home** a lot.

**4** girls' dolls **didn't break / broke** easily.

**5** people **set free / showed** the insects they caught.

**13** **Complete the sentences.**

> handmade   imagination   net   sewing   spare time

**1** You use a needle and thread to do _____.

**2** Most people do their hobbies in their _____.

**3** This candy isn't from a store or a factory. It's _____.

**4** Butterflies move quite slowly, so it's easy to catch them with a
_____.

**5** Children in the past had more _____ because they had to create
their own games.

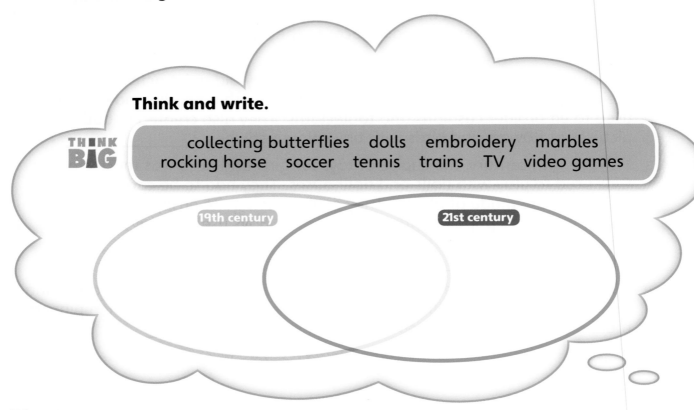

**Think and write.**

THINK
BIG

> collecting butterflies   dolls   embroidery   marbles
> rocking horse   soccer   tennis   trains   TV   video games

19th century          21st century

**14** **Read and choose the correct answers.**

**1** Butterfly collecting is a _____ than stamp collecting.

   **a** more interesting    **b** more interesting hobby

**2** Soccer is _____ tennis.

   **a** more popular than    **b** popular than

**3** Embroidery is _____ activity than sewing.

   **a** a more difficult    **b** more difficult

**4** Rats are _____ pets for children.

   **a** best    **b** the best

**5** The British Museum is probably one of _____ museums in London.

   **a** more interesting    **b** the most interesting

**6** Girls are usually _____ than boys.

   **a** organized    **b** more organized

**15** **Do you agree or disagree with the statements in 14? Write your comments. Use more, the most, and than.**

**1** _____

**2** _____

**3** _____

**4** _____

**5** _____

**6** _____

**16** **Read and complete.**

Did you know that...

**1** George Clooney is one of the _____ (rich) actors in Hollywood?

**2** Mawsynram in India has _____ (wet) weather than the U.K.?

**3** some of the _____ (tall) buildings in the world are in Dubai?

**4** scientists believe dolphins are _____ (intelligent) than rats and monkeys?

**5** raw vegetables are _____ (healthy) cooked vegetables?

**6** with more than 8.5 million visitors, the Louvre in Paris is the _____ (popular) museum in the world?

**17** **Read and compare. Write sentences.**

funny – *Despicable Me/Shrek/Ice Age*

creative – painting/stamp collecting/sewing

dangerous – skiing/mountain climbing/skydiving

small – Egyptian tortoise/coconut crab/bumblebee bat

hot – Greece/France/Saudi Arabia

tasty – chocolate/cheese/vegetables

**1** *Ice Age is funnier than Despicable Me, but Shrek is the funniest of all.*

**2** _____

**3** _____

**4** _____

**5** _____

**6** _____

**18** **Write questions. Then answer for you.**

> **Your school:**
> **1** Who is/old student/in your class?
> **2** Is/English/popular/other subjects?
> **3** What is/interesting class/in school?
> **4** Which sport/exciting/in school?
> **5** Are/classes/good/homework?

**1** _____ _____

**2** _____ _____

**3** _____ _____

**4** _____ _____

**5** _____ _____

**19** **Make phrases. Then complete the museum information.**

**1** underwater        sightings

**2** UFO        sculptures

**3** locks of        hair

**a**

Come in and leave
your _____
_____!

**b**

Come and read
information about
_____
_____!

**c**

Don't miss our
_____
_____!

**20** **Listen, read, and complete. When did a UFO land in Roswell?**

artists   experts   landed   marine   potter

1    This museum is in a national ¹_____ park. It has 400 wonderful sculptures. However, if you want to visit this place, you have to swim there. One of the ²_____ wanted his work to be part of the ocean life of the Mexican Yucatán Peninsula. You can see it displayed among plants, corals, and other marine life. Don't forget your swimming trunks or swimming suit.

2    Roswell, New Mexico, is famous for a UFO sighting in 1947. Many people believe a UFO actually ³_____ there. At Roswell's International UFO Museum and Research Center, you can't actually see any UFOs, but you can read the stories people tell about UFOs. The museum holds a festival every year. Many UFO ⁴_____ come to speak at the festival.

3    This is a museum that has pieces of hair. Each one has a person's name and the date it was cut. The hair is displayed in a cave in Turkey. The museum was started by a ⁵_____, and he displayed the very first lock of hair in his pottery shop. When he told people the story behind the hair, they wanted to leave their hair, too – and so the museum's life began.

**21** **Look at 20. Write UFO, Hair, or Underwater.**

1 There's only information here. _____

2 The things you see are part of nature. _____

3 They hold a festival each year. _____

4 It's in a protected area. _____

5 You see hair from different people here. _____

6 It belongs to one man. _____

**22** **Read and match.**

1 A person who makes cups and plates.

2 Describes ocean life.

3 A person who knows everything about a subject.

4 The rocky homes of tiny underwater animals – they're usually colorful.

5 Looking at things underwater with a mask and breathing tube.

a corals

b snorkeling

c potter

d marine

e expert

**Think of your own weird collection for a museum. Draw and then describe it.**

THINK
BIG

_____

_____

_____

_____

_____

_____

_____

**23** **Look and complete the informal letter. Use the words from the box.**

Beach View Hotel,
10 Pebble Lane,
Dorset,
DT1 XF2

August 12th, 2014
Dear
How are you?
Love,

1 _____

2 _____ Mia,

3 _____ I'm fine.

We're staying at the Beach View Hotel in Dorset, and it's great! I'm starting a shell collection. I got a lot yesterday. I went to the beach and saw them on the sand. The best one is beautiful and pink. I think it's my best shell yet. I'm having a great time on vacation. It's hot and sunny. Tomorrow we're going on a hike and maybe to the movies in the evening.

When I get home, I'll bring over my pictures and shells to show you.

4 _____

Beth

**24** **Write an informal letter to a friend. Tell your friend about a hobby. Here are some ideas:**

a healthy hobby     a creative hobby     a hobby that helps you learn

_____

_____

_____

_____

_____

_____

_____

**25** **Read and circle y and igh.**

fly    try    light

high    my    picture

cute    true

sky    fight    night

**26** **Underline the words with y and igh. Then read aloud.**

**1** Birds fly high in the sky.

**2** I watch the moon at night.

**27** **Connect the letters. Then write.**

**1** li          y          **a** _ _ _

**2** m          ght        **b** _ _ _ _ _

**3** fl          y          **c** _ _

164

**28** **Listen and write.**

Let's ¹_____,

Let's ²_____.

Let's ³_____

And ⁴_____

The ⁵_____

At ⁶_____!

**29** **Complete the dialogs with forms of bad, good, and ancient.**

**1**

**A:** Carol is _____ at chess.

**B:** Yes. But Henry is _____ Carol.

**A:** That's true. But I'm _____ of all.

**2**

**A:** Sean is a _____ singer.

**B:** I know! But Chris is _____ Sean.

**A:** Yes. But Brian is _____ singer of all.

**3**

**A:** Patty's Grandma is 90. That's really

_____.

**B:** Yes, but Marge's Grandma is _____

that. She's 98.

**A:** I know, and Randy's Grandma is

_____ of all. She's over a hundred!

**30** **Answer about your family. Write complete sentences.**

**1** Who's the best singer? _____

**2** Who's the worst singer? _____

**3** Who's the best dancer? _____

**4** Who's the worst dancer? _____

**5** Who's the oldest person? _____

**31** **Read and circle.**

**1** In the 19th century, dolls **was / were** made of china.

**2** Soccer was **give / given** rules for the first time.

**3** Girls **use to / used to** embroider cushions.

**4** Collecting butterflies **was / were** a popular hobby.

# unit 9

# Learning New Things

**1** **Solve the puzzle. Write the words in the boxes.**

**Across →**

**1**

_____ like a rock star

**2**

draw _____ books

**3**

_____

**4**

make a _____

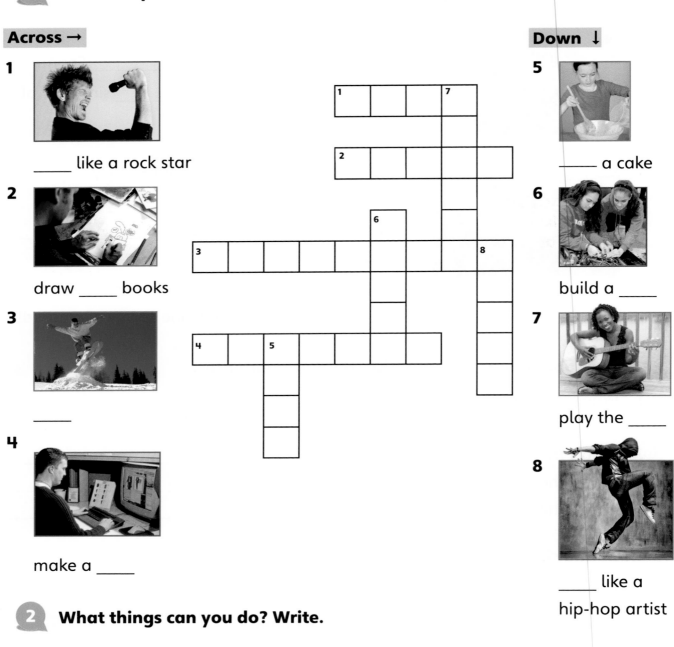

**Down ↓**

**5**

_____ a cake

**6**

build a _____

**7**

play the _____

**8**

_____ like a
hip-hop artist

**2** **What things can you do? Write.**

_____

_____

**3** **Listen and write. Use the words from the box.**

| bake draw learn show sing |
| skateboard speak |

### Learning Is Fun!

Do you know how to ¹_____?
    It's so great. It's so cool!
I can ²_____ you how to do it
    On Friday after school.

        It's fun to learn new things,
    Like how to ³_____
Or ⁴_____ or ⁵_____!
    I wish I had a lot more free time.
I would try to ⁶_____ everything!

    I'd like to learn to speak English.
    "It's hard!" my friends all say.
    But I think it's really interesting.
I'd like to ⁷_____ it well one day.

        Chorus

Do you want
to learn English?

Yes!

**4** **What activities are amazing, dangerous, and difficult? Write.**

1   I think it's amazing to _____

_____.

2   I think it's dangerous to _____

_____.

3   I think it's difficult to _____

_____.

**5** **Read. Then circle.**

## The Best in the Class

Christina and Sam are walking home from school. They see Jake, a boy from Sam's class, in the park. He's really good at playing the guitar. Sam can't play the guitar, but he'd like to learn. Jake tries to teach Sam to play the guitar. Sam isn't very good. Christina thinks Sam is terrible at playing the guitar.

**1** Jake is **in Sam's class / on the soccer team**.

**2** He's good at playing the **piano / guitar**.

**3** Sam **can / can't** play the guitar.

**4** He **would / wouldn't** like to learn how to play the guitar.

**5** Sam **is / isn't** very good at playing the guitar.

**6** **Write about you.**

I'd like to learn how to _____.

I'm good at _____.

I'm not very good at _____.

**THINK BIG**

**What happens next in the story? Use these ideas or think of your own.**

**1** Sam practices every day and learns how to play the guitar very well.

**2** Sam goes home and plays video games.

**3** Jake teaches Sam to play the guitar very well.

**7** Listen and stick. Then write.

learn to dance    learn to draw    learn to play tennis    learn to skateboard

1 _____

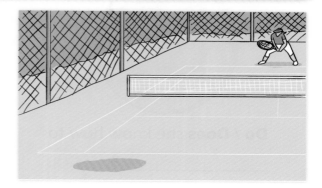

2 _____

3 _____

4 _____

**8** Look at 7. Complete the questions and write answers.

1 What would he _____

_____?

_____

2 What would she _____

_____?

_____

3 What would she _____

_____?

_____

4 What would she _____

_____?

_____

# Language in Action

**9** **Look. Then circle and complete.**

**1**

**Do / Does** she know how to

_____?

_____. Her cakes
taste delicious.

**2**

**Do / Does** you know how to

_____?

_____. But I can
play tennis.

**3**

Do **he / they** know how to

_____?

_____. They are
building one right now.

**4**

你好

Does **we / she** know how to

_____?

_____. But she speaks
English very well.

**10** **Write the questions and answers.**

**1** What does he think of snowboarding? _____ (fun)

**2** What do you think of making websites? _____ (boring)

**3** _____ They think it's difficult.
(dancing)

**4** _____ She thinks it's amazing.
(drawing comic books)

**11** **Read and complete.**

> bones   brain   joints   muscle   organs   skeleton

Our body is an amazing machine. The ¹_____ support the frame. They make up the body's ²_____, and they protect the important ³_____ inside our bodies. Different ⁴_____, such as our shoulders, knees, and elbows allow the frame to be flexible. These are covered with ⁵_____, which pulls the body in different directions. All of the different parts of the body are amazing, but none of them can work without one thing – the ⁶_____.

**12** **Read and number the paragraphs in order. Then listen and check.** 177

A   If the tennis player is good, she finds the correct position and hits the ball with <u>precision</u>. If the tennis player isn't very good, she misses the ball.

B   The tennis player's muscles all <u>contract</u> and make the bones and joints of her legs and arms move. Everything magically moves together.

C   A tennis player is standing at the end of a tennis court. She can see a ball coming toward her, and she wants to hit it.

D   The message travels down all the nerves and reaches the muscles. All the muscles get the message at the same time and get ready for <u>motion</u>.

E   The tennis player's brain creates a message. It says something like, "Hey, guys, this ball is coming my way – I really need to get into the correct position to hit it." Her brain sends the message to all her nerves, telling them that she wants to hit the ball.

**13** **Look at 12. Correct the sentences.**

**1** Your body tells your nerves that you want to move.

_____

**2** Your joints send messages to your muscles.

_____

**3** Your bones contract and get ready for motion.

_____

**4** Your organs and joints move together.

_____

**5** If you aren't a very good tennis player, you can hit the ball with precision.

_____

**14** **Look at 12. Match the three underlined words to a definition.**

**1** movement _____

**2** get smaller _____

**3** exactly right _____

**Think about your body. Complete the sentences.**

THINK
BIG

**1** Without _____

_____

_____.

**2** It's amazing that _____

_____

_____.

**15** **Read, complete, and match the offers.**

a _____ (I/put) some things in my bag if you like.

b _____ (I/give/ you) mine. I had that class this morning.

**1** Mom, where are my favorite socks?

**2** Wow, it's really hot in here.

**3** I don't have my geography book with me!

**4** My bag is really heavy.

**5** I want to play this game, but I don't know how.

c Really? _____ (I/open) a window, then.

d I don't know. _____ (I/help/ you) look for them.

e Never mind. _____ (I/show/ you) how to do it.

**16** **Read, choose, and complete the decisions. Use will.**

> ask Mom    buy    clean it    get him    give it    watch

**1** My bedroom is really messy. _____ on the weekend.

**2** I forgot about Tom's birthday. _____ a present later.

**3** I don't have any homework tonight. _____ a DVD instead.

**4** My bike is really small now. _____ for a new one.

**5** These T-shirts are both really nice, but I think _____ the red one.

**6** There's a cat in our backyard. _____ some milk.

# Grammar

**17** **Put the words in order.**

1  carry  I  'll  bag  your  you.  for

_____

2  buy  ball.  them  'll  a  new  I

_____

3  'll  I  eat  sandwich.  a

_____

4  won't  go  to  I  school  today.

_____

5  go  shopping  'll  today.  I

_____

6  learn  to  I  play  another  instrument.  musical  'll

_____

**18** **Complete the mini dialogs with your own ideas. Begin with I'll….**

1  **Friend:** I don't like this program. It's really boring.

   **You:** _____

2  **You:** Mom! I've cut my leg badly!

   **Mom:** Oh, no! _____

3  **Dad:** You didn't do well in that exam!

   **You:** _____

4  **Waiter:** Would you like to order something?

   **You:** _____

5  **Friend:** I'm going to a concert tonight. Do you want to come?

   **You:** _____

**19** **Read and complete.**

> average    exhibition    genius    Professional    talent

**1** _____ musicians play music for money.

**2** Tamara doesn't play really well or really badly, she's just _____.

**3** Greta is a great ballet dancer. She has a lot of _____ for dancing.

**4** There's an _____ of Aztec art at the Metropolitan Museum.

**5** Martin is only five, and he knows so many things. I think he's a _____.

180

**20** **Listen, read, and match. Put the sentences in the correct place.**

**A** He isn't just a genius. He's kind and helpful, too.

**B** Some experts think young children can't be professional artists.

**C** His talent for playing the guitar showed when he was just four.

1    Yuto Miyazawa was a professional musician when he was only eight years old! **¹** ☐ He was on TV and performed at Madison Square Garden. He even played with famous musicians like Ozzy Osbourne, Les Paul, and G.E. Smith.

2    Gregory Smith could read at two years old. He started college at ten, and by the time he was sixteen, he had several degrees, including in math. **²** ☐ Gregory uses his intelligence to help other people around the world.

3    Aelita Andre could draw before she could walk. People were interested in her paintings when she was just two. At the age of four, she had her first exhibition in New York. **³** ☐ Nevertheless, all her paintings sold out in the first two weeks.

**21** Look at **20**. Read and answer.

**1** Where did Yuto perform?

_____

**2** Who did Yuto play with?

_____

**3** How did Gregory get his degrees?

_____

**4** What happened at Aelita's exhibition?

_____

**22** Find and write the words from **20**.

**1** ngesiu        _____

**2** laettn        _____

**3** xebihtonii        _____

**4** frposesnoila        _____

**5** veagrae        _____

Imagine what Yuto, Gregory, and Aelita would say and write.

THINK BIG

**1** **You:** Would you like to learn how to play another instrument?
**Yuto:** _____

**2** **You:** Do you always like playing the guitar?
**Yuto:** _____

**3** **You:** What do you think of playing with famous musicians?
**Yuto:** _____

**4** **You:** Painting is really difficult. Do you think it's easy?
**Aelita:** _____

**5** **You:** Do you ever play with people your own age?
**Gregory:** _____

**23** **Look and complete the review. Use the words from the box.**

Reviewed by ¹_____

★ ★ ★ ★

## A Great ²_____ for Everyone!

*Kara Makes a Robot* is a ³_____ movie. I watched it last ⁴_____, and I really liked it. It's not a long movie. It's only about eighty minutes, but there is a lot of great ⁵_____ in it.

It's about a girl named Kara. She ⁶_____ a robot. At first, they're friends, but soon the robot starts doing silly things. It's very funny and exciting. I don't want to tell you too much. You should watch it for ⁷_____.

*Kara Makes a Robot* is a great movie, and I ⁸_____ it to everyone!

acting
builds
filmgirl123
funny
Movie
night
recommend
yourself

**24** **Write a review of a movie, book, or TV show you like.**

Reviewed by _____

_____

_____

_____

_____

_____

_____

_____

_____

_____

**25** **Read and circle ew, ay, and e_e.**

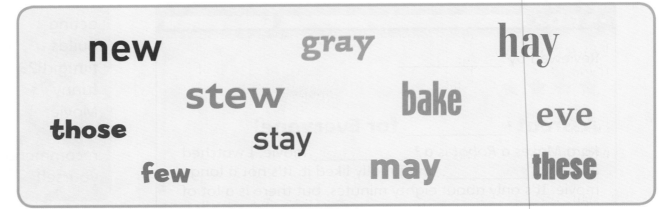

new

gray

hay

stew

bake

eve

those

stay

may

these

few

**26** **Underline the words with ew, ay, and e_e. Then read aloud.**

**1** I have a few of these gray scarves.

**2** Hey, they have a new board game.

**27** **Connect the letters. Then write.**

| | | | |
|---|---|---|---|
| **1** | th | ew | **a** _ _ _ |
| **2** | f | ese | **b** _ _ _ _ _ |
| **3** | n | ay | **c** _ _ _ _ |
| **4** | pr | ew | **d** _ _ _ |

**28** **Listen and write.**

185

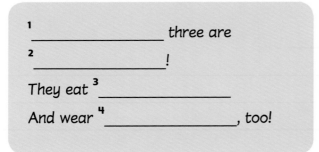

¹ _____ three are

² _____ !

They eat ³ _____

And wear ⁴ _____ , too!

**29** **Look at the chart. Write questions and answers.**

| What do they think of... ? | | | |
|---|---|---|---|
| Luisa | interesting | amazing | boring |
| Martin | interesting | cool | fun |

**1** What does Luisa think of drawing comic books?

_____

**2** _____

They think it's interesting.

**3** What does Martin think of singing like a rock star?

_____

**30** **Answer the questions in complete sentences.**

**1** Does Phil know how to speak Chinese? (no/but/speak Spanish)

_____

**2** What would they like to learn how to do? (build a robot)

_____

**3** What does she want to learn how to do? (dance like a hip-hop artist)

_____

**31** **Read and match.**

**1** What would you like for dessert?

**2** There's so much housework to do!

**3** Oh, no. I feel really sick.

**4** I'm going to a concert tonight.

**a** Taylor Swift? I love her! I'll come with you.

**b** Don't worry. I'll take the children to school.

**c** I'll help you finish it.

**d** I'll have chocolate cake, please.

**1** **Make guesses about Ben and ✓ the answers.**

Look at the happy and sad faces on Ben's calendar. Ben thinks some days are the best. He thinks some days are the worst.

**1** What's Ben like?

☐ friendly          ☐ funny

☐ good at chess     ☐ good at sports

☐ serious           ☐ smart

**2** What would Ben like to do?

☐ have a party      ☐ learn to snowboard

☐ learn to play chess   ☐ play video games

☐ watch fireworks   ☐ watch TV

| Sun | Mon |
|---|---|
| **Dec 31st** NEW YEAR'S EVE | **Jan 1st** ? |
| **7th** LEARN HOW TO | **8th** MEET FRIENDS SHARE COLLECTION |

**2** **Write on Ben's calendar. Write a hobby or things for Ben to learn on the tenth and the thirteenth.**

Make a guess about these two days.

**3** **Look at the calendar. Make guesses and write the answers.**

**1** What's Ben going to do on Monday?

_____

**2** What special day is on Saturday the sixth?

_____

# BEN'S CALENDAR

| Tues | Wed | Thurs | Fri | Sat |
|---|---|---|---|---|
| **2nd**<br>MEET FRIENDS<br><br>SHARE COLLECTION<br>😐 😐 | **3rd**<br>PRACTICE THE PIANO<br><br>☹️ ☹️ | **4th**<br>LEARN TO PLAY<br><br>😊 😊 😊 | **5th**<br>BAKE MOM'S<br>BIRTHDAY CAKE<br><br>😊 😊 😊 | **6th**<br>? |
| **9th**<br>PRACTICE SOCCER<br><br>☹️ ☹️ ☹️ | **10th**<br>?<br>_____<br>😊 😊 😊 | **11th**<br>MAKE A WEBSITE<br><br>😊 😊 😊 | **12th**<br>LEARN TO<br>PLAY BADMINTON<br><br>☹️ ☹️ | **13th**<br>?<br>_____<br>☹️ ☹️ ☹️ |

*The best!*

*The worst!*

**4** **What do you think of Ben? Would you like to be Ben's friend?**
**Write a letter about Ben to your parents. Begin:**

Dear Mom and Dad,

    I have a new classmate. His name is Ben. _____

_____

_____

_____

_____

_____

_____

| Who is **taller**, Chris or Tom? | Chris is **taller than** Tom. |
| --- | --- |

| | | |
| --- | --- | --- |
| old | ⟶ | old**er** |
| big | ⟶ | big**ger** |
| heavy | ⟶ | heav**ier** |

**1** **Read. Write the answers.**

**1** What is bigger? An elephant or a cat?

An elephant is _____ a cat.

**2** What is heavier? A notebook or a computer?

A computer is _____ a notebook.

**3** Who is older? Your grandmother or your aunt?

_____

**4** Who is taller? Your brother/sister or your father?

_____

**5** What is smaller? A baseball or a basketball?

_____

| My sister's hair is longer than **my hair**. | My sister's hair is longer than **mine**. |
| --- | --- |
| My sister's hair is longer than **your hair**. | My sister's hair is longer than **yours**. |

**2** **Circle the correct words.**

**1** **Your / Yours** backpack is heavy. But my backpack is heavier than **your / yours**.

**2** **Their / Theirs** hair is long. But my hair is longer than **their / theirs**.

**3** **Her / Hers** brother is younger than **my / mine**.

**4** **Our / Ours** classroom is bigger than **their / theirs** classroom.

**5** **My / Mine** friend is taller than Shaun's.

**6** **He / His** shoes are smaller than **her / hers** shoes.

| **Where** is | he/she | going after school? | He/She | is going to soccer practice. |
|---|---|---|---|---|
| **What** are | you | doing tonight? | We | are watching a DVD at home. |

**1** **Look. Write What or Where. Answer the questions.**

walk the dog

visit the dentist

**1** _____ is she doing after school today?

She _____.

**2** _____ are they going on Saturday?

They _____.

play video games

go to the shopping mall

**3** _____ is he doing tonight?

He _____.

**4** _____ are you going tonight?

We _____.

| **How often** does | he/she | have a guitar lesson? | **How often** do | you/they | go to school? |
|---|---|---|---|---|---|

**2** **Circle the correct questions. Write the answers.**

**1** **How often do / How often does** they do the dishes?

| Mon | Tues |
|---|---|

_____ a week.

**2** **How often do / How often does** she visit her cousins?

| Sun |
|---|

_____ a week.

| What **would** you **like**? | | | **I'd like** some soup. | | I'd like ⟶ I would like |
|---|---|---|---|---|---|
| What **would** | he/she | **like**? | He'**d**/She'**d** | **like** yogurt. | He'd/She'd like ⟶ He/She would like |

**1** Look. Write questions. Write the answers.

**1** What would she like for breakfast?

_____ eggs on toast.

**2** What _____ for a snack?

_____

**3** _____

_____ for dessert?

_____

## Favorite Food Survey

**1 Stacy:** eggs on toast for breakfast

**2 Martin:** steamed buns for a snack

**3 Stacy and Martin:** yogurt and watermelon for dessert

| Would | you | like to try some curry? | Yes, | I | would. | No, | I | wouldn't. |
|---|---|---|---|---|---|---|---|---|
| | he/she | | | we | | | we | |
| | they | | | he/she | | | he/she | |
| | | | | they | | | they | |

**2** Complete the dialog. Use the correct form of do, would, or like.

**1** **A:** Does Paula like Mexican food?

**B:** Yes, _____.

**A:** _____ she _____ to try some chili?

**B:** Yes, she would. She loves chili.

**2** **A:** Do you like hot drinks?

**B:** No, _____.

**A:** Would you like to try some lemonade?

**B:** No, _____. Thanks, anyway.

| I | | | I | |
|---|---|---|---|---|
| You | | | You | |
| He/She | **should** eat healthy food. | | He/She | **shouldn't** stay up late. |
| We | | | We | |
| They | | | They | |

**1** Write sentences with should and shouldn't. Use the ideas in the boxes.

**1** I have a fever.

_____

_____

| go to school today |
|---|
| rest |

**2** Her tooth hurts.

_____

_____

| go to the dentist |
|---|
| eat so much candy |

**3** Ted fell and hurt his knee.

_____

_____

| go to basketball practice |
|---|
| see the school nurse |

**4** Some children always feel tired.

_____

_____

| watch so much TV |
|---|
| get more exercise |

| I | | **myself.** |
|---|---|---|
| You | | **yourself.** |
| He/She | should take care of | **himself/herself.** |
| We | | **ourselves.** |
| They | | **themselves.** |

**2** Look at 1. Complete the sentences. Use herself, himself, themselves, or yourself.

**1** You should take care of _____.

**2** She should take care of _____.

**3** He _____.

**4** They _____.

> **How many** chimpanzees were there 100 years ago?

> There **were** more than one million. But now there **are** only about 200,000.

**1** **Complete the sentences.**

| Animal | Habitat | Population in the Past | Population Now |
|---|---|---|---|
| Mexican walking fish | streams and rivers in Mexico | a lot | almost none |

1 _____ Mexican walking fish ² _____ in Mexico now?

3 _____ a lot of Mexican walking fish in Mexican streams and rivers in the past?

Now, ⁴ _____ almost none. In the past, ⁵ _____ a lot.

> **Why** are chimpanzees endangered?

> They're endangered **because** people are moving into their habitat.

**2** **Answer the questions. Use the information from the box and because.**

> their habitat's polluted
>
> people are keeping them as pets

**1** Why is the Egyptian tortoise endangered?

It's endangered _____

_____.

**2** Why are Andean flamingos endangered?

_____

_____.

| | |
|---|---|
| **Did** people **have** cars in 1950? | Yes, they **did**. |
| **Did** people **have** cars in 1900? | No, they **didn't**. They traveled by horse and buggy or by train. |
| Before TV, what **did** people **use to do** for entertainment at night? | They **used to listen** to the radio. |

**1** **Read. Then answer the questions. Use did or didn't, do or don't, use or used.**

### Then and Now

1930s – People usually listened to the radio. They didn't own TVs.

Today -- People sometimes listen to the radio. Most people watch TV.

1950s – People wrote letters by hand.

Today – Many people write letters on the computer.

1970s -- Young people played outdoor games, like hide-and-seek.

Today – Many people, young and old, play video games.

**1** Did people listen to the radio years ago?

Yes, _____ because they didn't have TVs.

Do people listen to the radio now?

Yes, _____, but they usually watch TV.

**2** Did people use to write letters on the computer a long time ago?

_____

Do they write letters on the computer now?

_____

**3** Before video games, what _____ young people

_____ to do for fun?

They _____ to play hide-and-seek outdoors.

| When are | you | going to have the party? | I | am going to have it on Monday. |
| | | | We | are going to have it on Monday. |
| | they | | They | |
| When is | he/she | going to visit Grandma? | He/She | is going to visit her next month. |
| Are you/they going to visit Grandma on the ninth? | | | Yes, on the ninth. | |
| Is he/she going to visit Grandma on the fifth? | | | No, on the ninth. | |

**1** **Complete the questions and answers. Use going to and the words from the box.**

fourth     second     third     twenty-second

**1**

give a present July 2nd

When _____ your dad

_____ to your mom?

On the _____.

**2**

watch a parade April 22nd

When _____ they

_____ a parade?

_____

**3**

wear different clothes July 4th

When _____ you

_____ different clothes?

_____

**4**

have a party July 3rd

When _____ you

_____ a party?

_____

**2** **Look and write.**

**1** fourteenth _____    **2** eighth _____    **3** thirtieth _____    **4** first _____

| | |
|---|---|
| Katie is a **good** chess player. | My brother's paintings are **bad**. |
| Katie is a **better** chess player **than** Jeff. | My sister's paintings are **worse than** his. |
| Katie is **the best** chess player in the class. | My paintings are **the worst** of all. |

**1** **Look and complete the sentences.**

**1** **(big)**

| | Number of shells |
|---|---|
| John | 85 |
| Mike | 250 |
| Sally | 1000 |

John loves collecting shells. His collection is ¹_____. Mike's collection is ²_____ John's. But Sally has ³_____ in the whole class. She started when she was six.

**2** **(good)**

| | Wins |
|---|---|
| Ella | 10 |
| Stephanie | 4 |
| Tania | 6 |

Ella is good at video games. She is ¹_____ in the class. Stephanie is a ²_____ video game player. But Tania practices a lot. She's ³_____ Stephanie.

**3** **(bad)**

| | Losses |
|---|---|
| Bears | 5 |
| Tigers | 3 |
| Lions | 4 |

The Bears, the Tigers, and the Lions are popular baseball teams, but they are not having a good year. The Bears team is ¹_____ of the three teams this year. The Lions are ²_____ than the Tigers. But the Tigers are pretty ³_____, too.

**2** **Look and match.**

**1** He's good          **a** good at climbing trees.

**2** She's not very      **b** are bad at soccer.

**3** They               **c** at music.

| Do you **know how to play** the piano? | | | Yes, I do. / No, I don't. | | |
|---|---|---|---|---|---|
| What would | you | like to learn how to do? | I'd | like to **learn how to play** the piano. | |
| | he/she | | He'd/She'd | | |
| | they | | They'd | | |

**1** **Read. Then answer the questions. Use the words from the box.**

> bake a cake    make a website    sing like a rock star

**1** Jeff and Tina are going to have singing lessons next year. What would they like to learn?

_____

**2** Sue loves cakes. She's having a baking class now. What would she like to learn?

_____

**3** Bryan loves computers. He is having a web-design class now. What would he like to learn?

_____

| What do you **think of** ballet? | I think it's boring. |
|---|---|
| What does he **think of** hip-hop music? | He thinks it's cool. |

**2** **Complete the dialogs.**

**1** **A:** What do _____

_____ ?

**B:** I _____ it's cool.

**2** **A:** What does _____

_____ ?

**B:** She _____ it's a lot of fun.

## – 5 questions –

**Listen and look. There is one example.**

Getting Ready for School

Time Susan woke up: _____7:30_____

1 What she's having for breakfast: _____

2 How she's getting to school: _____

3 What homework she did for today: _____

4 What she's doing after school: _____

5 Her chore for today: _____

# Young Learners English Practice: Listening B

## – 5 questions –

 **Listen and look. There is one example.**

What is Martin's hobby?

**A** ☐

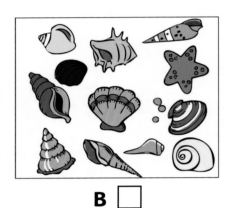

**B** ☐

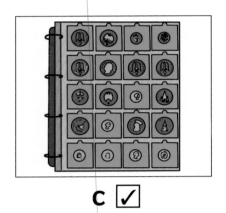

**C** ☑

1 What does Jane like doing?

**A** ☐

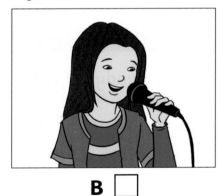

**B** ☐

**C** ☐

2 Which instrument does Anthony know how to play?

**A** ☐

**B** ☐

**C** ☐

3   What is the boy's favorite sport?

   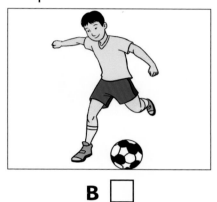   

A ☐          B ☐          C ☐

4   What is the class going to do?

A ☐          B ☐          C ☐

5   What are they going to do later on?

A ☐          B ☐          C ☐

# Young Learners English Practice: Reading & Writing A

## – 6 questions –

**Look and read. Write *yes* or *no*.**

## Examples

The dog knows how to ride a skateboard.  _____ yes _____

The little boy knows how to ride a bicycle.  _____ no _____

**Questions**

1 The girls know how to play tennis. _____

2 The man can sing well. _____

3 The bird knows how to talk. _____

4 The woman is going to cross the street. _____

5 A parade is coming. _____

6 You can see fireworks in the sky. _____

# Young Learners English Practice: Reading & Writing B

## – 6 questions –

**Look and read. Choose the correct words and write them on the lines.**

a slide

chess

a guitar

a birthday cake

actors

a comic book

a video game

a robot

## Example

This is a game you play on a computer
or TV screen.

_a video game_

## Questions

1 This is a musical instrument with strings.

_____

2 These are the people in a play or movie.

_____

3 This is a game you play on a board by
moving pieces.

_____

4 This is a book that tells a story with
pictures and speech bubbles.

_____

5 This is a machine that does work for
people.

_____

6 This is something people often eat on
their birthdays.

_____

# Young Learners English Practice: Reading & Writing C

– 5 questions –

**Read the text and choose the best answer.**

**Paul is talking to his friend Vicky.**

## Example

**Vicky:**  Hi, Paul. What are you doing?

**Paul:**  A  I'm fine, thank you.

B  I had a party.

(C)  I'm making a cake.

## Questions

1  **Vicky:**  What is it for?

**Paul:**  A  It's for my parents' anniversary.

B  On the last day of the year.

C  It's two days until Mother's Day.

**2 Vicky:** Would you like some help?

    **Paul:**    A    OK. What time?

                   B    Sure, I would love to.

                   C    That would be great.

**3 Vicky:** What would you like me to do?

    **Paul:**    A    You can beat the eggs.

                   B    No, thanks, I don't like eggs.

                   C    Two eggs are better than one.

**4 Vicky:** Should I use this bowl?

    **Paul:**    A    It's not as big as the other one.

                   B    No, use the bigger one.

                   C    Because I like it.

**5 Vicky:** And then what are we going to do?

    **Paul:**    A    Mix everything and put it in the oven.

                   B    Flour, eggs, and milk.

                   C    The oven is hot now.

**6 Vicky:** When will it be finished?

    **Paul:**    A    Every once in a while.

                   B    In about an hour.

                   C    It lasts a long time.

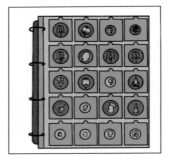

# Extra Verb Practice

| Base Form | Simple Past | Base Form | Simple Past |
|-----------|-------------|-----------|-------------|
| ask | _____ | fly | _____ |
| _____ | baked | _____ | got |
| be | _____ | give | _____ |
| _____ | began | _____ | went |
| bring | _____ | grow | _____ |
| _____ | built | _____ | had |
| buy | _____ | hear | _____ |
| _____ | called | _____ | helped |
| catch | _____ | hit | _____ |
| _____ | celebrated | _____ | held |
| change | _____ | hope | _____ |
| _____ | came | _____ | kept |
| cook | _____ | kill | _____ |
| _____ | cut | _____ | knew |
| destroy | _____ | learn | _____ |
| _____ | did | _____ | left |
| draw | _____ | like | _____ |
| _____ | drank | _____ | listened |
| drive | _____ | live | _____ |
| _____ | ate | _____ | looked |
| explain | _____ | lose | _____ |
| _____ | fell | _____ | loved |
| feed | _____ | make | _____ |
| _____ | felt | _____ | met |
| fight | _____ | move | _____ |
| _____ | found | _____ | needed |

| Base Form | Simple Past | | Base Form | Simple Past |
|-----------|-------------|---|-----------|-------------|
| perform | _____ | | tell | _____ |
| _____ | planned | | _____ | thought |
| play | _____ | | throw | _____ |
| _____ | put | | _____ | traveled |
| read | _____ | | try | _____ |
| _____ | realized | | _____ | turned |
| rest | _____ | | understand | _____ |
| _____ | rode | | _____ | used |
| ring | _____ | | visit | _____ |
| _____ | ran | | _____ | waited |
| say | _____ | | wake up | _____ |
| _____ | saw | | _____ | walked |
| sell | _____ | | want | _____ |
| _____ | sent | | _____ | washed |
| sing | _____ | | watch | _____ |
| _____ | sat | | _____ | wore |
| skateboard | _____ | | worry | _____ |
| _____ | slept | | _____ | wrote |
| snowboard | _____ | | yell | _____ |
| _____ | spoke | | | |
| stand | _____ | | | |
| _____ | started | | | |
| stay up | _____ | | | |
| _____ | swam | | | |
| take | _____ | | | |
| _____ | talked | | | |

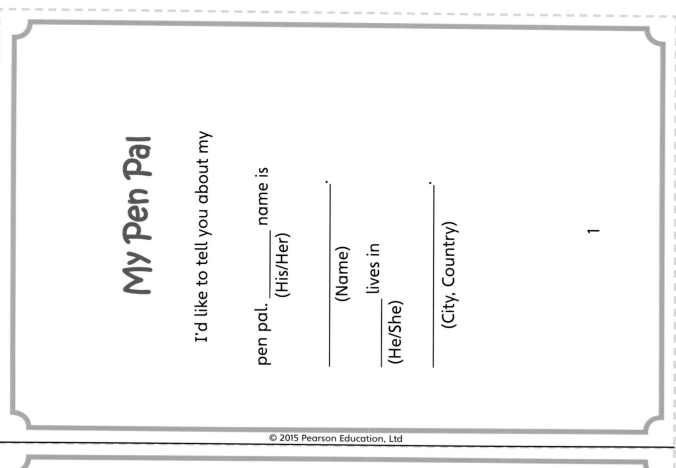

## My Pen Pal

I'd like to tell you about my

pen pal. _____ name is
          (His/Her)

_____ .
(Name)

_____ lives in
(He/She)

_____ .
(City, Country)

1

He/She likes _____
                  (activity)

and _____ .
       (activity)

_____ wants to visit me here
(He/She)

in _____ , too!
   (where I live)

4

**Card 2**

_____ loves eating
(Name)

_____ food.
(adjective)

_____ favorite dish is _____.
(His/Her)                              (food)

(He/She) eats it _____.
                        (how often)

I'd like to try it, too!

**Card 3**

_____ has _____ hair.
(Name)              (adjective)

_____ hair is _____.
(His/Her)                    (adjective)

(He/She) is really _____.
                          (adjective)

sore eyes

ate too much candy

have a cold

sore throat

have a cough

used the computer too much

stomachache

played too many video games

allergies while playing outside

sneezing

drank too much lemonade

watched too much TV

# SCHOOL TALENT SHOW

# Wednesday, May 9th

# 6:00 P.M.–7:30 P.M.

# School Auditorium

# Vote for the best talent!

# Sign up to perform by Friday, May 4th.

# 4 My BIG ENGLISH World

My name: _____

My age: _____

My address: _____

My family: _____

ME

FOLD

# ENGLISH
## AROUND ME

Look around you. Paste or draw things with English words. Write *everyday words* and *sentences*.

Everyday Words

Everyday Sentences

Henry's Chocolate

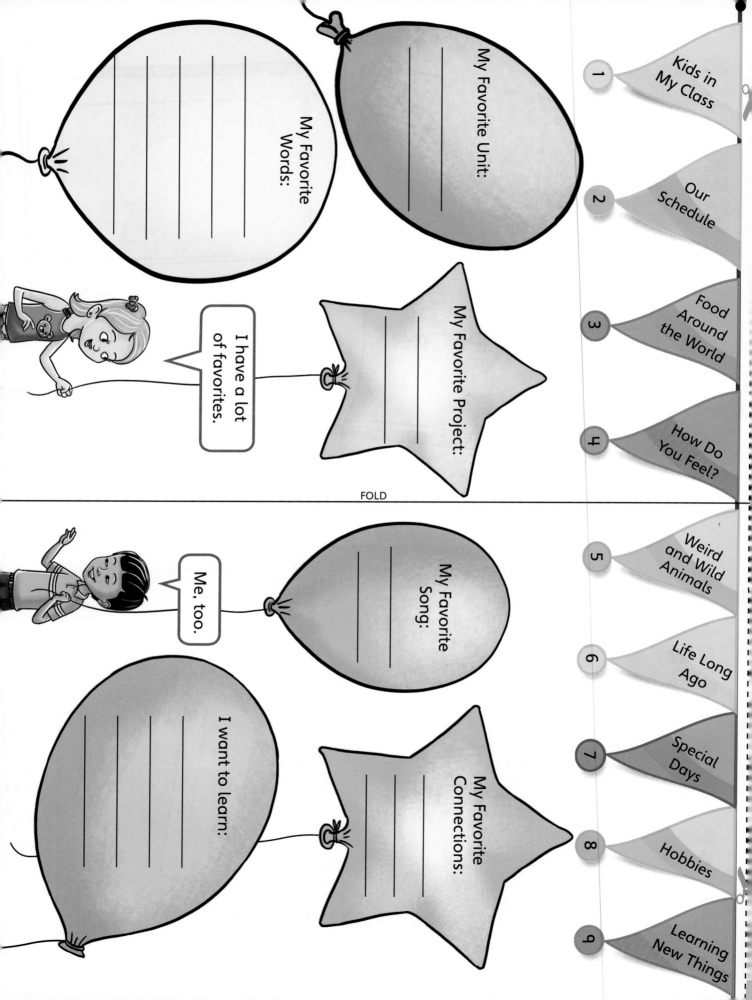